ABORIGINAL PLACE NAMES

of Mount Banda Banda was responsible for this name.

Bandup (W): large lake.

Bandyup (W): place of black swans.

Bangalee (N): sandy beach. Original name for Shoalhaven River.

Bangalow (N): from *bangalla*, a low hill; a kind of palm tree.

Bangan (Q): wooden spear.

Bangaroo (N): native bear.

Bangaum (Q): snail.

Bangingoo (Q): man running.

Banyam (N): sleeping lizard. Now North Lismore.

Banyo (Q): ridge.

Banyula (V): many trees.

Baradine (N): red wallaby.

Barathawomba (Q): put it on top.

Baratta (V): shag.

Barbigal (N): a frosty place, little frost.

Barcoo (Q): ice on the water.

Bardinnerrang (N): small water.

Bardoc (W): wild fellow.

Bareemal (M): a large waterfall.

Barellan (N): meeting of the waters.

Barmera (S): from *Barmeedjie*, the name of an Aboriginal tribe in the vicinity.

Barnawatha (N): from *barnawoodther*, deaf and dumb.

Barow (Q): magpie.

Baroota (S): name of the tribe which had its permanent encampment at Baroota Creek.

Barra (Q): grubs.

Barraba (N): see *Taengarrahwarrawarildi*.

Barreenong (N): wattle flower.

Barrenjoey (N): young kangaroo.

Barrine, Lake (Q): a crater lake. The name has some connection with a local legend.

Barringum (N): fish die in the water.

Barringup (W): watering place.

Barwon (N): from *barwum* or *bawon*, meaning great, wide, awful river, or river of muddy water. Somewhat surprisingly a contradictory meaning has been given as good water, because the water in the river was always good to drink. There were three places of this name in New South Wales, each name probably being conferred because of some legend or event which occurred in that particular neighbourhood.

Baryulgil (N): a species of large lizard.

Batagup (W): bare rock.

Bathanny (Q): good day.

Bathillboro (Q): spring on top of a mountain.

Battunga (S): place of large trees.

Beabula (N): two black cockatoos.

Bean Bean (N): bellbird.

Bearing (W): stop there.

Becchal (Q): where a man was speared.

Bedberry (W): big crocodile.

Beddi (V): a steep place.

Beeburing (Q): king parrot.

Beerburrum (Q): parrot.

Beereegan (N): the place of the quail. There were several places of this name in New South Wales.

Beeroogoon (N): the creator of shellfish.

Beerriwera (N): make haste, hurry.

Beerubri (N): a hole in a tree.

Beetaloo (S): springs and creeks.

Bega (N): large camping ground; or from *bika*, beautiful.

-beit (V): suffix meaning lake, used in Victoria.

Belar (N): the forest of oak trees. This tree was common in many parts of New South Wales and the name appeared frequently, sometimes in conjunction with other words, e.g. Belaradah, place of the forest oaks. While the word *belar* had currency over a wide area, the following part of the name sometimes varied with the language of the different tribes.

Belaradah (N): forest oak trees, from *belar*, oak and *dah*, place of.

Belardoo (W): white land on the coast.

Belaring (W): a swamp surrounded by tea-tree.

Belbucanina (W): a native bird called by the early settlers a squeaker.

Belingbak (Q): a tree with a large lump or growth on the trunk.

Belladoonia (S): red rock. There is a red granite outcrop at this place.

Bellambi (N): no.

Bellarinya (Q): mistletoe.

Bellata (N): kangaroo.

Bellbourie (N): a reed-covered lagoon with scrub-lined creeks draining into it.

Bellbudgerie (Q): no good.

Belleringah (N): from *beelahingar*, a creek with crayfish. From *beelah*, creek; *ingar*, crayfish.

Belongil (N): inlet of the sea.

Beltana (S): running water; or possibly from *peltana*, possum skin.

Belubula (N): stony river; big lagoon.

Benalla (V): from *benalta*, musk duck.

Benbullen (N): high, quiet place.

Benelong Point (N): Benelong was a young Aboriginal who was captured by Governor Phillip, and well treated. He was later taken to England and met the King.

Bengalla (N): ornaments. The Aborigines did not affect many ornaments, apart from painted decoration of their skins, but shells, feathers, necklaces of seeds and other ornaments were used in some tribes.

Bengaccah (Q): ordinary kind of place without any special features.

Benhennie (N): dry land. Now Camden.

Benomera (N): holes in a hill. Fish River or Jenolan Caves.

Benowa (Q): bloodwood tree.

Beom (Q): paddymelon.

Bepera (W): place where a woman ran away when the moon rose.

Berangin (W): kangaroo skin cloak. While tribes in the interior and in the hotter regions wore no clothes, those who frequented colder districts were glad of the protection of roughly-made skin cloaks during inclement weather.

Beregegama (N): a lagoon shaped like a horse-shoe, therefore a name of comparatively recent vintage. Now Horse-shoe Lagoon.

Bereowaltha (N): to get down.

Bergalin (W): burial ground.

Berieel (N): a place surrounded by rocks which are overgrown with rushes.

Bermagui (N): canoe, or better, canoe with paddles. Bark canoes were impelled by this means, and also the heavier dugout canoes of the northern regions. On an early plan the name appears as Permageua.

Berrabri (N): to make haste, hurry.

Berree (Q): mangrove tree.

Berri (S): a bush that grows plentifully in this district.

Berrico (N): a hollow place.

Berrima (N): to the south.

Berrimbillah (N): green birds, kingfishers.

Berringoo (Q): to cry.

Berriwere (N): from *bherwerre*, to hurry; large expanse of water.

Berriwerri (N): a crossing place.

Berriwilliman (Q): green parrot.

Bertical (V): country where the quandong tree grows.

Bettuyungaanysung (W): to clean fish.

Biala (N): I understand.

Biama (N): Baiame, or Byamee, q.v., was the Great Spirit. He was supposed to have remained at this place for some time and to have imparted his knowledge to the Boomi people of the Kamilaroi tribe.

Bibanup (W): white rocks.

Bibbakine (W): flat-topped hills.

Bibbenluke (N): place of birds; big look-out.

Bibboorah (N): a burning hill-like fire. Now Peak Hill.

Bibil (N): white-leaved boxtree, a common tree in many parts of New South Wales and the interior, often appearing in variants such as *bimbil* and *bimmil*.

Bidaminock (W): a place which is haunted by the spirits of the dead; a place inhabited by snakes.

Billabong Creek (N): an effluent from a river, sometimes separated from it, sometimes being joined again at time of flood; also used loosely as a lake or pool. The name is in common use in New South Wales, sometimes appearing in the form *billabung*. *Billa* is a pool or reach of water, *bung* or *bong* means dead.

Billagoe (N): possibly from *billegow*, sandpiper.

Billanbri (N): a creek where rushes grow.

Billenargill (N): country between a lake and the sea.

Billeroy (N): running water, creek.

Billinooba (Q): place of parrots.

Billinudjel (Q): place where parrots are plentiful; home of the king parrot.

Biloela (N): cockatoo. An early name of this place was Cockatoo Island, and it is said that the original name was *Warrienbah*.

Bimberdong (W): hillside.

Bimbi (N): from *bimbimbi*, place of many birds.

Bimblegumbie (N): the sound made by a spear as it whistles through the air when thrown from a woomera.

Bimpi (Q): neck.

Binalong (N): towards a high place.

Binbilla (Q): interlacing vines used in making windbreaks and huts. Such primitive shelters were all that the Aboriginal needed to shelter him from the weather when camping. This place is now the Botanic Gardens, Brisbane.

Binda (N): deep water.

Bindowan (Q): grasshopper.

Bingamon (N): sandhills where a few pine trees are growing.

Bingarra (N): creek.

Bingarrah (W): trees struck by lightning.

Binge (N): belly.

Bingeering (W): a large gully with a stream which dries up in summer time.

Bingeraba (Q): saltwater crossing place.

Biningyarrah (W): an itch, usually referred to as *chip chip*.

Binkenbar (Q): a small tortoise.

Binnaburra (N): beech trees; place of white beech trees.

Binnawan (N): burial ground.

Binnum (S): plenty of she-oaks.

Bintamiling (W): many red flowers.

Binya (N): a cutting; a mountain.

Biraganbil (N): place of leeches.

Birdup (W): plenty of birds.

Biroo (Q): hand.

Birool (N): I spear you.

Birribi (Q): freshwater crossing place.

Birriebongie (N): from *birrie-bungie*, shag.

Biwongkalla (N): place of the red tea-tree (*biwong*).

Bobledigbie (N): a name which dates back only to the days of white settlement. The meaning seems to be "a kick on the posterior", and the story is that the owner of the run meted out this treatment to one of his "boys" when he disobeyed an order. With a sense of fun the imaginative Aboriginal stockmen immediately gave a fitting name to the place where the incident occurred.

Bobra (N): singing.

Bocobble (N): sheep jumping. In the early days of settlement the sheep had to pass through a gap at this place and jumped about as they struggled to get through.

Bodalla (N): a number of interpretations have been given for this name, one being that it comes from *bowdall*, to toss a child up and down in the arms. Other meanings have been given, such as several waters, you run hard, and haven for boats. At one time the place was popularly known as Boat Alley, one of the amusing corruptions of an Aboriginal word.

Bogabilla (N): rivers and swamps; and again comes the same explanation as for *Bogan*, q.v.

Bogan (N): the birthplace of a notable headman of the local tribe.

Bogandilla (Q): big water.

Bogan Gate (N): an inexplicable meaning put forward is "birthplace of a king". However the derivation given under *Bogan* probably provides the correct answer.

Boggabri (N): there are two possible explanations: from *boorgaburri*, emu and young, and from *bukkibera* or *bukkibri*, place of creeks. The *Australian Encyclopaedia* favours the latter.

Bogobogalong (N): plain with creeks running through it.

Bogong (V): large moth; place infested with fleas.

Bogonk (N): a large moth

which is plentiful in the Snowy Mountains in summer.

Boiboigar (N): apple tree. Now Rosebank.

Boigon (N): place of the wattle tree.

Boikonumba (N): place of ferns, from *boikon*, fern.

Boilyup (W): water bubbling in a soak.

Boin Boin (N): mosquitoes.

Bojalup (W): rocky place.

Bokaring (W): wearing of skins.

Bolan Bolan (V): lory parrot.

Bolaro (N): man with boomerang.

Bolga or **Bolgar** (N): see *Bulgar*.

Bollup (W): pool of water.

Bombala (N): meeting of the waters.

Bombery (N): seaweed.

Bombo (N): from *Thumbon*, the name of a renowned headman and warrior born in this district.

Bondi (N): from *boondi*, the sound of tumbling waters or of seas rolling in on a beach.

-bone (N): suffix used in New South Wales, meaning the place of. It is in frequent use.

Bong- (V and N): see *Bung-*.

Bongaree (Q): the name of a young Aboriginal who accompanied Flinders to Moreton Bay. Also known as Bribie Island.

Bong Bong (N): from *bung bung*, much swamp. *Bung* means swamp; *bung bung*, much swamp. It can also be rendered as plenty of water about and, by association, many frogs.

Boningwee (V): burnt hole in a pine tree.

Bonnonee (Q): a big river.

Bonyi (Q): from *bunya*, a native pine tree. The season of the eating of the ripe bunya pine nuts was an important occasion amongst Queensland tribes. Now the Blackball Range.

Boobajool (N): child, or young of any animal.

Boobigan (Q): flooded ground.

Boobijan (Q): ashes.

Booborowie (S): round water hole.

Booderoo (W): stony land.

Boodgerakarta (W): large hill.

Boodup (W): a smoky place.

Boogo Boogo (N): pretty, beautiful.

Booiyana (N): sandy country. The root word *booi* implies bending, giving way, or pliable. The sandpiper was called *booiyoowaalwaal*, the one like soft or sandy ground; *booibirrang* was a toy boomerang made of bark, and therefore soft and not likely to cause damage when used by a child.

Booka (N): standing. The word often appears in names with a qualifying suffix.

Bookabie '(S): brackish water.

Booka Booka (N): from *booga booga*, stink stink, many bad smells.

Bookbook (V): night owl.

Bookinoragh (Q): water-hen.

Bookoola (N): owl.

Bookoor (Q): crane.

Bookra (Q): cold weather.

Boolaroo (N): many flies; place of many flies.

Boolbadah (N): a place where a camp was made and then abandoned.

Boolbilly (N): bullock.

Booleroo Centre (S): plenty of mud and clay. The word "centre" was added because it is in the Hundred of Booleroo.

Boolgun (S): much; many.

Booligal (N): big swamp; windy place; place of the flooded box trees.

Boolooinahl (N): dark side of mountain. Now Blue Nob.

Boomgarla (Q): to kill.

Boomi (N): dark brackish water.

Boomi (W): piece of wood; stick.

Boomooderie (N): man throwing a nulla nulla or club.

Boona, Mount (N): swampy country.

Boona or **Boonah** (Q): from *buna*, bloodwood tree.

Boonboolong (N): place or home of the Evil One. There are many legends about the greatly-feared Evil One, a spirit who had the ability to turn himself into various forms.

Boondarn (N): from *boonahookdarn*, the lawyer vine.

Boonderabbi (W): good watering place.

Boonderoo (W): stony place.

Boondine (W): thick scrub.

Boongun (N): brush turkey.

Booningi (Q): place where bags are hung up for drums. Apart from the drone pipe, the only musical instruments possessed by the Aborigines were striking sticks to mark the rhythm of dance and song, and in a few places a type of drum, usually consisting of a rolled skin beaten with the hand. This name seems to imply that a similar type of instrument was hung from the branch of tree and beaten with the hand or a stick.

Booningie (Q): place where hair was cut.

Boonoo Boonoo (N): poor country with no animals to provide food.

Boonooloo (W): a spring with a plentiful supply of water.

Boonoona (N): white ground.

Boonthno (N): wool.

Boorabbin (W): a chain of water holes.

Booradabie (W): three big rocks.

Boorageree (N): a woman's fishing ground.

Booragul (N): summer.

Boorah (Q): kite hawk.

Booral (N): big; large.

Booran (Q): south wind.

Boorang (N): mountain where the wattle trees grow.

Boorebuck (N): a *bora* ground, i.e. a prepared place where initiation ceremonies are held and therefore a sacred place.

Booreebiddy (N): big belly.

Boorgidjeagoorah (Q): watershed.

Boorinine (W): turtle.

Boorlahboorloo (Q): dry; place where grass does not grow; never green.

Booroodabin (Q): place of oak trees. At one time they grew abundantly in this locality.

Booroogarrabowyraneyand (N): head of a saltwater creek, from *booroogarra*, salt water; *bowyra*, head of a creek; *neyand*, top. Now the Clarence River.

Booroogum (N): land crab.

Boorooma (N): dingo.

Boorowa or **Burrowa** (N): plain turkey.

Boorpah (N): the circle inside which *bora* or initiation rites

were performed. It has also been rendered as a "rendezvous". In 1900 the Sydney Registrar-General suggested that it would be an appropriate name for the Federal Capital.

Boorraiberrima (N): to struggle violently.

Boorthanna (S): from *boorthe-boorthanna*, a bushy plain.

Bootha (Q): white.

Boothaguo (N): to smell you.

Bootill (Q): flowers.

Booungun (N): place where there are swarms of blowflies.

Booyah (Q): the sound of small birds.

Booyamurra (N): a shapely ankle.

Booyong (N): ironwood tree.

Booyooarto (S): hill belonging to Booyoolie (probably a totemic ancestor). Now Mount Herbert.

Booyoolie (S): swirling up of a cloud of smoke.

Booyup (W): large stone.

Bora Pine and **Bora Ridge** (N): also spelt *Borah* and *Borrie*. An initiation ground.

Borallin (W): plenty of prickly trees.

Borambil or **Boranbil** (N): this name is also connected with *bora*, the ceremonial ground, and has been defined as either a place near the initiation ground, or a projecting root of a tree.

Borambola (N): see *Borambil* above.

Boranga Bore (N): big water hole. An artisian bore at this place reached a depth of 4,000 ft.

Borandijup (W): hill.

Boranup (W): swamp.

Boree (N): fire; a species of yarran tree.

Borrika (S): a stranger's hut.

Borup (W): boys.

Bouderee (N): large fishing ground. Now Jervis Bay.

Boui Boui (N): many mosquitoes.

Boun (N): a native bird. Now Wallis's Plain.

Boundahalcarra (W): nesting ground of the eagles.

Bouradie (N): to knock the teeth out. This was part of the manhood rites that all boys had to undergo in many parts of the country, to prove their courage and readiness for adult life. In some places girls also were subjected to the ordeal at the time of the puberty ceremonies.

Bourbah (N): from *borabung*, the place of initiation ceremonies.

Bourbong (Q): dead hill which spat at one time.

Bowral (N): from *boorool*, high, or large.

Bowyum (N): a sleeping lizard.

Boylegerup (W): a large plain.

Boyup (W): place with a smoky appearance.

Bralgon (V): native companion.

Bran Bran (N): locusts.

Bredlaboura (N): formerly *Billbabourie*, a good place.

Breeza (N): from *biridja*, a flea.

Brewarrina (N): the usual meaning given is the fisheries, sometimes simply fishing. Other meanings recorded include acacia clumps, and a native standing. However, one student has said that although the name was given to the native fishing places in the Darling River, the true translation is more likely to have come from *birie*, wild gooseberry. If this is so the name would mean the place where wild gooseberries grow.

Brewitataandee (V): the place where fresh snow had fallen.

Brewongle (N): camping place.

Brigalow (V): native companion.

Brigalow (Q): wattle tree.

Brimbago (S): big swamp.

Brinawa (N): place where rock lilies grow.

Bringagee (N): breast to breast.

Bringelli (N): unobtainable.

Broolgang (V): magpie lark.

Broomoing (W): plenty of shade

Broula (N): trickling water.

Browie (N): oak scrub.

Bruthen Bruthen (V): from *Brewon*, an evil spirit who appeared here and gave his name to the place, which is pronounced *Brewdthan*.

Brymedura (N): nest of a mallee hen.

Bubbracowie (S): water hole where pigfaces grow.

Bublara (W): turkey.

Bucca Bucca (N): a crooked creek.

Buckajo (N): running water.

Buckalow (N): a small lake.

Buckawackah (N): to crawl on hands and knees, probably to commemorate an occasion when a kangaroo or other animal was stalked by a hunter.

Bucking (N): place where cooking is done.

Bucklebone (N): see *Bugilbone*.

Budda (N): where the *budda* or *budah* trees grow.

Buddabone (N): place of the *budah* trees. Now Butterbone.

Buderim (Q): honeysuckle.

Budgerahgum: soft hair. Now Lionsville.

Budgeree (N): good; nulla nulla wood.

Budgeribong (N): big tree.

Budgerie (Q): very good.

Budgimby (N): smell of the turtle.

Budjewy (N): young grass.

Budla (Q): ice.

Budumba (Q): high, stony country.

Bugabada (N): maggots; stinking.

Bugar (Q): shield.

Bugilbone (N): place of the death adder. Now Bucklebone.

Bugwanada (N): stunted pine with spreading branches.

Bujerup (W): large swamp.

Bukartilla (S): swimming place. Now Hahndorf.

Bukkulla (N): tall black stump.

Bulahdilah, Bulladeela, or **Bulahdelah** (N): meeting of the waters, junction of two creeks; big creek; big rocks; good camping place.

Bulba (N): an island.

Bulberry (Q): quail.

Buldthery (N): plover; plovers' nest.

Bulga, Bolga, Bolgar or **Bulgar** (N): single mountain; big mountain. There are several places bearing this name, in particular a mountain peak near Carcoar, and another south of Port Hacking.

Bulga Bulga (N): many men; mountains.

Bulgan (N): a shield.

Bulgandramine (N): from *bulgandirramine*, a man with a boomerang in his hand. *Bulgan*, boomerang; *dirra*, hand; *mine*, man. Other meanings given are: throwing a boomerang with the hand; man on a mountain; man with a shield.

Bulgandry (N): man holding boomerang. See above.

Bulganinup(W): running spring.

Bulimba (Q): see *Tugulawa*.

Buljarngennee (W): place where small fish are caught.

Bulkee (Q): fat. The fortuitous pun seems almost too good to be true.

Bulkeewhirlbarr (Q): poor.

Bulkirra (N): the back of a man or an animal. The name is used metaphorically of mountains.

Bulla (N): see *Bulli*.

Bulla- (N): a prefix meaning two, appearing in several names.

Bulla Bulla (V): four hills; four creeks.

Bulladelah (N): a big creek.

Bullakibil (N): a bullfrog.

Bullamwall (V): two spears. The name was given to two mountains.

Bullatop (N): two hills.

Bullawhay (N): flame tree. Now Bexhill.

Bullawie (N): night; dark.

Bullen Bullen (N): big fight; lonely place; very quiet.

Bullengen (N): handsome.

Bulli (N): from *bulla*, two mountains. These are the two mountains Keira and Kembla. Other renderings are

between the hills; place where the Christmas bush grows; white grubs. However there seems little doubt that it means two mountain peaks. There are several places with *bulla* as part of the name. When it appears as *bulla bulla* it probably means four peaks.

Bulligema (Q): troopers dispersing the Aborigines.

Bullina (N): named after the Aboriginal tribe which lived at the mouth of the Richmond River.

Bullion (W): plenty.

Bullo (Q): a sheep.

Bullockina (Q): big mob of cattle.

Bullon (Q): narrow place.

Bulong (W): a place where water was drunk through a piece of bark.

Bumbaldry (N): an onomatopoeic word to describe the noise made when men and women jump into the water.

Bumboah (N): a large tuft of grass.

Bumbulla (N): to go away.

Bumgobittah (N): plenty of flying sqirrels.

Bumgum (N): hard ground.

Bunagan (Q): old woman climbed high up in the tree. It was often the task of women to climb trees to rob honey nests and even to chop lizards out of holes in branches.

Bunbibilla (N): a cloak made of possum skin.

Bundaberg (Q): a hybrid name. It has been recorded that the members of the Bunda tribe adopted a surveyor and gave him their own tribal name. The town was later called Bunda's Town or Bundaberg.

Bunda Bunda (N) : see *Banda Banda*.

Bunda Bunda (S): Aboriginal name for the Nullabor Plain, which is not a native word, but named by the surveyor and explorer Alfred Delisser in 1866 as a modification of *nullus arbor*, no tree.

Bundaleer (S): among the trees.

Bundall (Q): a prickly vine; a crooked creek.

Bundanoon (N): place of deep gullies.

Bundarra (N): a large kangaroo.

Bundarryuron (N): long water. Now Bellinger River.

Bundi (N): fighting with nulla nullas.

Bung- and **Bong-** (N and V): usually a creek which flows only in winter and spring and dries up in the summer.

Bungancoor (W): many swamps.

Bungara (Q): sickness.

Bungaree (S): my country.

Bungarra (Q): spring with the remains of an old fire close by.

Bungawahl or **Bungwahl** (N): an edible, bulbous swamp root sometimes called *uki*.

Bungawalbin (N): swamp where rooted weeds grow. See *Bungawahl* above.

Bungawarrah (W): granite rocks and shallow water.

Bungawitta (N): plenty of flying squirrels and possums.

Bung Bung (N): many meanings can and have been given to this name: big swamp; much swamp; many springs of water (from *bung* or *bong*, a spring); plenty of riflebirds (from *bung*, riflebird); plenty of water; long swampy stretch of country.

Bungega (N): to chop.

Bungendorf (N): big hill rising from the plain; place of gum blossom.

Bungiebomah (N): to hit and break, from *bungie*, to break; *bomah*, to hit.

Bungleboori (N): a crooked bend. In this case a bend in the Tocumwai Creek.

Bungledool (N): little woman.

Bunglegumbie (N): broken limb.

Bungobaine (N): flying squirrel alighting on a tree.

Bungonia (N): creek which flows only in the rainy season.

Bungoona (V): sandy creek.

Bungulla (Q): spear.

Bungulla (N): black bream.

Bungumme (N): hard ground.

Now called Sandilands.

Bungunya (Q): deserted shelter or hut.

Bungwahl (N): see *Bungawahl*.

Bungyancoor (W) : many swamps.

Bunna (N): rain.

Bunna Bunna (N): plenty of rain (literally rain, rain). Big lagoon.

Bunnacower (V): plain where emus make plenty of dust.

Bunnerong (N): sleeping lizard; swamp.

Bunora (S): long distance; far away.

Bunyacubbol (N): stony ridges.

Burgooney (N): ants tunnelling in sandy soil.

Buribuca (N): water lilies.

Burnamagoo (N): the name of the local tribe.

Burra (S): said to come from the Burra Burra Creek, *burra burra* meaning great, great, or very great. It may also mean very many, or very large stones. However, the original name was probably *Kooringa*. The manager of the Burra mines said that the name was derived from a Hindustani word.

Burra (N): hill ants; big fellow; stone.

Burrabira (N): stones under water. Now Sow and Pigs.

Burraburoo or **Burraburra** (N): steep hills.

Burradoo (N): many brigalow trees.

Burraga or **Burrajaa** (N): bitter swamp water; rocky water; a bandicoot.

Burragah (N): a meeting place. Now Little Bay.

Burraganbar (N): wind. Now Camera.

Burraganee (N): a boomerang. Now Gorge.

Burragorang (N): from *booroon*, a small animal; *gong*, going to hunt; therefore going to hunt a small animal; a tribe which lives in a valley where there is plenty of game. It is also said to be the name of a tribe which wore a pin through the nose as an ornament.

Burrahbaa (N): the shape of a ship. Now Montague Island.

Burrandong or **Burrangong** (N): hunting place; native bear; from *boorongong*, a hunting ground.

Burrawang (N): there were several places of this name and it is not unlikely that they bore different meanings, such as: wild ducks; red kangaroo; anything, such as an animal, that could run very fast. *Burrawang* was the name of a native palm which grew very abundantly in some parts. The large seeds had a pungent flavour and were very popular. They were crushed to powder, mixed with water, and baked as cakes in the ashes of a fire.

Burrayangatti or **Burragunbutti** (N): dead stinging tree.

Burrell (W): the Aboriginal name for Perth, meaning not known.

Burren Junction (N): big creek.

Burrendah (N): place of the swan.

Burri (N): to be quick; to make haste; to hurry.

Burri Burri (N): distant hill.

Burrill, Lake (N): from *burrul*, wallaby.

Burrimul (N): place of blowflies.

Burringbar (N): from *burring*, boomerang. This particular weapon was not used for throwing, but was really a striking stick.

Burrinjuck (N): rugged-topped mountain; precipitous mountain.

Burrowa: see *Boorowa*.

Burrumbeit (V): freshwater lake.

Burrygup (W): the home of a supernatural monster.

Buruda (Q): from *boorooda*, forest oak.

Burungule (S): the name of a legendary hero who conquered an evil spirit at this place.

Bussiwarrallwarrall (N): an earthquake.

Buthia Buthia (Q): plenty of small birds.

Butho (N): grass.

Buttaba (N): hill on the edge of a lake.

Byamee (N): the supreme spiritual being or Great Spirit of many of the tribes of eastern New South Wales. Other forms of the name were *Biami, Baiami, Baiamai*, etc.

Bygalorie (N): red kangaroo.

Bywong (N): big hill.

C

Cabbaga (Q): a garden.

Cabbagee (Q): night.

Cabdo (Q): a baby.

Caboolture (Q): from *cabul*, carpet snake.

Caboon (Q): a lyre bird.

Cabramatta (N): from *cobramatta*, the home of the *cobra*, or land jutting out where the *cobra* is found. One account says that *cobra* is a grub, another that it is a bivalve.

Caddajin (N): many large round stones on an open plain.

Cadgee (N): from *cudgee*, very good.

Caggaramabill (Q): porcupine. Now Mount Gravatt.

Cajildry or **Cajildri** (N): from

cajil, smoke; *dri*, place of. Place where smoke is rising.

Calaberthaniga (W): well off for firewood.

Calamia (W): the place of fire.

Calannie (W): place where white stone for spear head is obtained.

Calawathie (W): nothing with which to make fire.

Calbertine (W): soft quartz hill.

Calboonya (Q): a lyre bird.

Calca (S): stars.

Caling (N): mussel.

Callan (Q): sparrow hawk.

Callanna (S): named after a legendary kangaroo which came to this place to drink.

Callemondah (N): plenty of hills.

Caloola (N): place where a battle was fought.

Caloundra (Q): beautiful headland.

Caltipurti (N): from *calte*, emu; *purte*, eggs. Emu eggs.

Caltowie (S): water hole of the sleepy lizard.

Calume (W): black wattle tree.

Calwalla (N): water running out.

Calyeeeruka (N): dingo tracks.

Cambalup (W): bulrush swamp.

Cambee (Q): blankets.

Cambewarra (N): from *cambe*, fire; *warra*, a high place or mountain. The name may therefore be translated as mountain of fire, or fire

coming from the mountain. The Nowra tribe in this region had a tradition that smoke once belched forth from the mountain, and subsequent investigation showed that there was a seam of coal there which had apparently been ignited at some time in the past.

Camira (N): wind; reeds used for making dilly bags. The dilly bag was the carry-all of the Aboriginal. Into it went his or her few possessions with the exception of the coolamon and fighting and hunting weapons. It was more usually carried by women who were required to transport the household goods on walkabout, leaving the men free to rush off to the hunt as soon as an animal was sighted.

Camooweal (Q): high wind.

Canberra (ACT): from *nganbirra*, a meeting place. In 1826 Joshua Moore wrote to the Colonial Secretary advising that the land which he intended purchasing was at *Canberry*, and the deed was issued to him at this place. Other conjectures are that the name comes from *kaamberra*, and that this or *nganbirra* mean a woman's breasts.

Candiup (W): plenty of bush rats.

Camphallup (W): large pool of still water.

Canindboary (Q): marriage.

Cannawigra (S): pathway made of sticks over muddy ground.

Canobolas (N): the name of this extinct volcano comes from *coona*, shoulder; *booloo*, two, and therefore means two shoulders. The two "shoulders" are the twin peaks Old Man and Young Man Canobolas.

Canomie (Q): where the north wind blows. Now North Koppel Island.

Canowie (S): from *kanyaowie*, water hole in the rock.

Canowindra (N): a home.

Capemount (W): thick rushes growing over a soak.

Carabobala (V): leather-head or honey-sucker.

Carara (Q): clear ground.

Carathee (N): sister.

Carathool (N): native companion.

Carawah (N): plenty of birds sit down here.

Carawatha (N): the place of pines. Now Finley.

Carbanup (W): plenty of large flag rushes.

Carbinup (W): plenty of turtles in a freshwater swamp.

Carbuckin (W): place of the burnt tree.

Carcoar (N): frog, crow, or laughing jackass. According to one authority the name comes from *cahcoah*, kookaburra.

Cargelligo, Lake (N): from *kartjellakoo*. *Kartjell*, a coolamon; *akoo*, he had; therefore, he had a coolamon. A coolamon is the bark or wooden dish used to carry water, seeds, and other possessions. Another translation is simply lake.

Carkginginup or **Carkigugingup** (W): favourite camping place.

Carmumdagual (Q): backbone.

Carra Carra (N): over there.

Carramolane (W): caves in a hill.

Carranaggin (W): many permanent springs.

Carrarthang (W): beds of red ants.

Carrican (Q): sparrow hawk.

Carripan (W): to dig holes.

Cartalacoolah (Q): a water hole between two sandhills.

Cartee (N): mother.

Cartmeticup (W): a little hill in the shape of a man's head.

Carvie (W): needle tree.

Carwoola (N): the meeting of waters on the plain.

Casino (N): dogwood tree.

Catherko (Q): a calf.

Catthalalla (Q): the long creek. Now Cliffdale Creek.

Cawana Swamp (Q): a turtle.

Ceduna (S): a water hole.

Ceolgerk (W): a swan.

Cererch (W): a black cockatoo with a red tail.

Ceron (W): a red gum tree.

Chargem (N): a baby. Now Tatham.

Chargin (N): young children.

Charra (S): emu droppings.

Chatterup (W): a dingo.

Chepearrup (W): plenty of tall grass growing here.

Chidna (Q): track of a foot.

Chilgerrie (N): a green-headed ant.

Chinchilla (Q): from *jinchilla*, cypress pine.

Chinna (Q): a foot.

Chinocup (W): plenty of devils.

Chinogan (N): low behind and high in front. The name is descriptive of the mountain.

Chipalee (Q): a whistling duck.

Chittennup (W): place of the white flower. The roots of this plant were an important article of diet in this region.

Choongurra (N): from *choongurrabannarindearn*, pelican corroboree ground.

Choonnanging (W): a broken waddy.

Chounboon (N): black clouds.

Chubie (Q): a crab.

Chullundie (S): water, or some reference to water.

Chulora (N): flour. This was the flour obtained by the Abo-rigines by grinding the seeds of grass and other plants between flat stones before mixing it to a paste and making.

Chumparia (N): Blue Mountain parrot.

Chungandoonmoneybiggera (M): from *chungan*, lightning; *doonmoney*, struck; *biggera*, ironbark tree. An ironbark tree struck by lightning. There is a similar name elsewhere in New South Wales *Chungandoonmoneychallie*, a tree struck by lightning.

Clergin (V): magpie lark.

Clybucca (N): a crooked tallow-wood tree.

Coacatocalleen (N): drinking water.

Coalbaggie (N): swimming or bathing place.

Coatneal (N): a flat in the shape of a half moon.

Cobakh (N): a tree, the leaves of which are used to poison water in a water hole and stupefy the fish, thus making them easy to catch.

Cobar (N): from *cuburra*, burnt earth or red clay, used to paint the body. Another explanation of the name is that it was the native pro-nunciation of the English word copper.

Cobargo (N): grandfather.

Cobbadamana (Q): caught by

the head. The name has some connection with the legend of an Aboriginal woman who had an accident during childbirth.

Cobbal (N): a carpet snake.

Cobbenbil (N): many insects.

Cobbi (N): a wasps' nest.

Cobbora (N): from *koburra*, the head.

Cobdogla (S): the meaning of the word is not known, but it is said to be an exclamation used by a young Aboriginal woman when she saw one of the first settlers making a sketch of the Murray River from the tailboard of a cart.

Coblinine or **Coblinnie** (W): a river in the shape of a man's belly.

Cobranaraguy (N): a headband.

Cocamittanewannie (N): bald red sandhills.

Cockamongar (W): a crows' nest.

Cockelup (W): place where a man was burnt.

Codobine (W): where a man removed the heart from another.

Coedie (Q): a boy.

Coerabko (S): meeting place of the tribes. Now Morgan.

Cogin (N): north.

Cohuna (N): native companion.

Colac (V): rosella parrot.

Colah, Mount (N): anger.

Colane (N): the name of a tree.

Collarendebri or **Collarenebri** (N): place of many flowers.

Collaroy (N): the junction of two creeks; a large reed which grows in swamps.

Collendina (N): curling waters, from *collie*, water.

Collie (N and W): *collie* is the term for lagoons and large water holes, and appears in many compound names, e.g. *Colliyu, Colliburl, Collieblue,* etc., and in modified forms, as in *Collendina*.

Colliet (N): sweetheart, lover.

Colliup (W): watering place.

Collymongle (N): very long lagoon.

Comarra (N): a cut sinew.

Comba (N): a root word with many compounds, usually applied to water holes, lakes, etc., e.g. *Combadello, Combadri* and in other names such as *Coombah, Coombak, Combok*.

Combo (N): a terror for women.

Combok (N): to hold water.

Comboyne (N): a female kangaroo; women.

Comeacome (Q): devil-devil.

Comoo (Q): water.

Condannican (N): a flying fox.

Condercutting (W): a parrot.

Condobolin (N): hop rush.

Condowie Plains (S): good water.

Congha (W): a stone axe.

Conmurra (S): a stony hill.

Connay (N): a digging stick.

Coobah (Q): a large white yam.

Cooberpedy (S): white fellow's hole in the ground. The name was given by the curious Aborigines after it was discovered to be an opal field. The miners took refuge in dugouts and holes in the ground to escape from the heat.

Coobowie (S): much water.

Coobungo (Q): dead trees.

Coobyaangar (Q): mullet.

Coocarah (N): a fern growing on a tree.

Coochiemudlow (Q): red rocks.

Coochimudlow (Q): red clay.

Coochin Coochin (Q): reddish colour.

Coodging (N): red ochre or clay used by the Aborigines for painting bodies and sacred objects.

Cooeburra (Q): a curlew.

Coogee (N): from *koocha* or *koojah*, rotten seaweed. Also translated stinking, or the bad smell caused by decayed seaweed washed ashore.

Coogongoora (N): a laughing jackass.

Coogoorah (N): a reedy swamp.

Cookadinya or **Cookardinia** (V): a giant kingfisher.

Cookamobila (N): a creek with many tree stumps.

Cooki or **Crooki** (W): swamp here.

Cool- (N): a component of many compound names in New South Wales, usually meaning rock adder.

Coolabah (N): a species of eucalyptus commonly called *coolabah* by white people.

Coolabulling (W): a bag; plenty.

Coolac (N): a native bear.

Coolah (N): angry; vexed; junction of two streams.

Coolamon (N): the common Aboriginal term for the dish made of wood or bark, used for many purposes such as carrying water, seeds (and mixing them with water to make flour), carrying babies, and small objects. It was made from a swelling or excrescence growing on box trees, and was therefore applied to the excrescences as well as to the dish made from them. Natural water holes found in level country sometimes had the appearance of such dishes and were also called *coolamon*.

Coolangatta (Q): fine or splendid look-out or view. Other meanings given are elbow hill or large hill. There is yet another conjecture to the effect that the name comes from a vessel wrecked here in 1846.

Coolawin (N): a big koala bear.

Coolbaroomookoo or **Cool-**

buroomookoo (N): lucky fellow fire.

Coolbart (W): a magpie.

Coolberry (N): an emu.

Coolgardie (W): named after a boy who found a water hole at this place.

Coolibullup (W): place infested with kangaroo ticks.

Coolingup (W): a swamp where spearwood grows; a watering place.

Coolong (N): wombat goes in.

Coolongolook (N): towards the high places.

Cooloni (N): liquor.

Cooloon (N): a tick.

Cooloongatta (N): the highest land; a good look-out.

Coolootai (N): rock adders here.

Coolowyn (Q): a beech tree.

Coolringdon (N): a black swamp intersected by streams.

Cooluddagadden (W): white sand.

Coolum, Mount (Q): see *Nindherry*.

Coolumbla (N): water from a hill. Now Rosebrook.

Coolyaganah (W): to cut up a man. This was supposed to refer to a feast, but it should be noted that the Aborigines were not cannibals, and the only occasions when human flesh was eaten was as a token only and of a symbolic,

ritualistic nature, and even then only in certain tribes.

Coolyaron (N): a big sandhill.

Cooma (N): from *coombah*, big lake, or open country. Other meanings are one, sand bank.

Coomaling (W): plenty of possums.

Coomalwangra (W): talking possums.

Coomandook (S): the place took its name from country some miles away, the name of which was *coomandook*, country belonging to the enemy.

Coombah (N): a baby boy.

Coombabah (Q): a pocket of land.

Coombak (N): to hold water (the name of a water hole).

Coombie (N): a drum or percussion instrument of some kind used to decoy emus.

Coombimbah (Q): a hunting ground.

Coombullnee (N): tail of a dingo. Now Kenny's Creek.

Coomburra (N): a spirit.

Coomealla (N): the meeting place of several streams.

Coomel (W): a possum.

Coomera River (Q): from *kumera kumera*, the name of a fern which grew near the village of Upper Coomera. Also rendered as blood.

Coominyah (Q): where is the

water? Formerly Bellevue.

Coomooroo (S): small seeds for making flour.

Coomoorooguree (N): place where the edible *coomoorooguree* grub is found in grass trees.

Coompagimpa (Q): a water hole in the bed of a river.

Coomunderry (N): a small, narrow flat.

Coonabarabran (N): an inquisitive person.

Coonalpyn (S): a woman without children.

Coonamble (N): from *goonamble*, plenty of dirt; bullock dung.

Coonatta (S): a tree which exudes manna.

Coonawarra (S): honeysuckle rise.

Coonbar (Q): day.

Coonderabbri (W): a good watering place.

Coondoo (Q): a death adder.

Coondoondah (Q): a hat.

Coonerang (N): a small possum.

Coonkie (N): place of the evil spirit.

Coopernook (N): an elbow.

Cooplacurripa (N): plenty of mosquitoes.

Coora (W): a bush kangaroo.

Cooraburrama (N): a bunyip or water monster.

Coorain (N): wind.

Cooran (Q): Moreton Bay ash tree.

Cooranggoorah (N): a grass tree.

Coori (N): flowers.

Coorong, The (S): from *kurangh*, neck, the name given to a narrow lagoon.

Cooroombong (N): a creek with a stony bed.

Coorparoo (Q): a ground dove. The name resembles the note of the cooing bird.

Coorrabin (W): a spring which had never been known to fail.

Coorumbene (N): a pretty place.

Cootamundra (N): from *gooramundra*, meaning swamp, low-lying place, and also turtles.

Cootapatamba (N): where eagles drink.

Cootha, Mount (Q): the honey of native bees.

Cooyong (V): a bandicoot.

Coraki (N): from *kurrachee*, the mouth of a river; heat; plain turkey. Another explanation was given by Bob Turnbull, an Aboriginal at Purfleet to Roland Robinson and recorded in *The Man who Sold his Dreaming*. Turnbull said Frank Jock, another Aboriginal, allowed the Council to put in a charge of explosive to form a quarry in the mountain on payment of ten dollars and two bottles of rum. Thus he sold his dreaming, and the local tribesmen called the place *gurrigai*, or blowing up the mountain. This was corrupted in time to Coraki.

Corama (V): a plain on which emu feathers are found.

Coraperena (N): a straight line.

Coreen (N): end of the hills; last of the hills.

Corella (S): a white or pink parrot.

Corobimilla (N): a tree struck by lightning.

Corowa (N): from *currawa*, a pine tree from which gum was obtained to fasten the heads to spears. Other meanings given are rocky river or rocky rivers.

Corramulling (W): a flat rock.

Corranewarran (V): the home of squirrels.

Corrobora (N): a spring on a mountain side.

Coulta (S): from *koolto*, the name of a nearby spring.

Cowabbie (N): the name given to cows when first seen.

Cowan (N): big water; uncle.

Cowar (N): staghorn ferns.

Cowardine (W): a place with no water.

Cowgongie (N): a place where there are certain trees from which hieleman or shields were made.

Cowieaurita (S): a yellowish-brown liquid. Now Jacob's Creek.

Cowra (N): rocks.

Cowrang (V): brown gravel.

Coyelgee or **Cooyelgup** (W): a water snake.

Coyinguine (N): an island.

Cringila (N): the name was bestowed when the Aborigines of the Kiama district came here to obtain pipeclay to paint their bodies prior to setting out on fighting expeditions.

Croajenalong: see *Krowathun-koolung*.

Croajingalong (N): looking eastwards; high plains.

Croki (N): from *groki*, a toad-fish.

Cronulla (N): either from *kurranulla*, small pink shells, or from *koorungnulla*, choked up. An earlier name for this district was *Gunna-matta*, meaning beach and sandhills.

Crooki (W): see *Cooki*.

Crudine (N): a goanna.

Crumbana (Q): a man dead in camp.

Cubaway (N): a large bush fire.

Cubbacubbah (N): green.

Cubbine (W): good hunting.

Cubbletrenock or **Cubbletrenak** (N): a narrow stony gorge, applied to the head of the Manning River.

Cubery (N): hunger.

Cubtahpooliman (Q): an

Aboriginal policeman.

Cudal (N): flat.

Cudgee (V): a very good place.

Cudgegong (N): red hill. Red clay from this place was used in body decoration. Another explanation is that the name comes from *giddy giddy*, a bird.

Cudgelo (N): a hollow log or tree.

Cudgen (N): another word for red clay, or red. See *Cudgegong*.

Cudlee Creek (S): from *kudlee*, a dingo. Another theory is that the place was first called Chudleigh Creek.

Culgoa (N): running through; returning.

Culing (N): a mussel shell.

Culkineborough (W): the mouth of a river.

Culkinewarinebinelup (W): a place where palms grow profusely.

Cullanine or **Cullemine** (W): fire.

Cullenbone (N): the meeting of the waters.

Cullenbullen (N): lyrebirds. Also claimed to be the place of many waters.

Cullengoin (N): blood and water.

Cullengoral (N): the meeting place of the waters in the Gulgong district.

Cullingral (N): a deep water hole in the Merriwa district.

Cullya (N): an emu.

Culmara (N): ferns.

Cumbalum (N): a place where flathead fish are caught.

Cumbingum (N): a runaway woman.

Cumble (N): a wild turkey.

Cumboogie (N): gum leaves; sweet scented gum.

Cumbooglecumbong (N): from *cumbooglecaban*, plenty of manna, or sweet food. *Cumboogle*, the sweet deposit on gum tree leaves; *caban*, plenty of.

Cumboyne (N): a broken-topped mountain.

Cumbulam (N): see *Cumbalum*.

Cummara (N): blood.

Cundiah (Q): to walk about.

Cundle Town (N): *cundle*, a native plant with fruit which resembles a carrot in appearance.

Cundugyup (W): a very good spring of water.

Cundumbul (N): big mountains.

Cundumully (Q): a native companion.

Cuni (N): a digging stick.

Cunygera (Q): plenty of pelicans on the water.

Curban (N): jammed between two trees.

Curbanmah (N): a rough, narrow passage.

Curbollie (N): to sew a cloak.

Curdalup (W): a swamp.

Curnoomgully (N): from *cur-noom*, stumps; *gully*, place of: therefore a place where there are many stumps.

Curra- (N): prefix meaning a spring of water.

Curra (N): a heavy cold.

Currabubula (N): two forked trees. Mitchell called it Carrabolila, which his men turned into Terrible Bay.

Curracobark: an open space.

Curragundi (N): water hole; place of many spiders; place of many mosquitoes. It can be understood that the name for a water hole and for mosquitoes could well be synonymous.

Curragurra (N): heavy stones.

Currambine (N): heaps of rock.

Currambul or **Curranbul** (N): a white swamp. The name was given on account of the small trees which grew amongst the rocks and gave this appearance to the swamp.

Curramulka (S): from *curre*, emu; *mulka*, deep water holes. Emus came down to drink, fell in the hole, and were speared by the hunters.

Currikee (N): turtles.

Currimundri (Q): the wing of a flying fox.

Curringbung (N): from *curring*, sticks; *bung*, standing: bent sticks standing here. Now White's Swamp.

Curroon (N): fog on top of a mountain.

Currumbin (Q): a species of pine tree.

Currumbungee (N): a wallaby. Now Pumpkin Swamp.

Currumburra (V): a giant king-fisher.

Currunghi (N): bark shed by gum trees.

Curtiupah (N): a kangaroo rat.

Curtmerup (W): a good place for the bulbs which are known to the Aborigines as *cuties*.

Cussigungaringhi (N): a place where eels were caught in a net.

Cussrunghi (N): the place of the white gum tree from which the bark is peeling. Now Jerseyville.

Cutana (S): a water hole on the plain.

Cutchup (V): a rocky plain with pine trees growing there.

Cuttebarley or **Cuttibarley** (N): goodbye.

Cuttyguttygang (N): plenty of parrots here; to sit down.

D

Dadgra (W): flesh.

Dagamgurra (Q): plenty of pelicans.

Dakkabin (Q): a grass tree.

Damolock (W): twenty-eight parrots.

Dandaloo (N): probably from *dundulla*, *bundilla*, or *bundulla*, which are the words for hail amongst various tribes in New South Wales.

Dandarragan or **Dandaraga** (W): very good country.

Dandenong (V): high.

Dangin (W): a place where emus were plucked. Usually the head was removed and the whole body was placed in the oven, the feathers and skin being dragged off before eating.

Daping (W): a deep water hole.

Dapto (N): a lame person.

Darel (N): blue sky.

Darile (W): rosella parrot.

Darkin (W): black rocks.

Darling (W): been a hill.

Darlingup (W): a swamp.

Daroobalgie (N): to jump in the water.

Darra, Derra, or **Durra** (N): thigh. There were many places of this name and others derived from the same root and with the same meaning in New South Wales and southern Queensland.

Darraring (W): a spear barb.

Daymar (Q): red ridge.

Debing (Q): a mosquito.

Deeragun (Q): an ear.

Deerangoomar (N): *deeran*, mountain; *goomar*, a plant with a fruit shaped like a pineapple. The mountain where the *goomar* grows.

Delgibo (Q): from *dugil*, a stone; *bu* (an abbreviation of *bubai*), standing. Stone standing up.

Deleanberry (N): west wind.

Delungra (N): a water weed.

Demondrille (N): probably derived from a word meaning where many large reeds are found. The plant had a strong stalk from which light spears were made.

Dendendaloom (Q): a wren.

Deniliquin (N): from *Denilakoon*, the name of the leader or headman of a local tribe who is said to have killed the first white man he met. The place was first known as The Sandhills.

Deningup (W): been a large hill.

Dennawan (N): the foot of a large emu.

Derra (N): see *Darra*.

Derrilin (N): falling stars.

Dewitt (N): plenty of blowflies.

Dhoonygooroonthie (N): sunset.

Dhoonywulgunny (N): sunrise.

Dhoora Dhoora (N): a day's walk.

Dilga (N): a broken or splintered tree.

Dilgon (N): like a moon.

Dilladerry (N): from *doolahdoolahderry*, the place of many logs. The name has been rendered as, "Oh see what a lot of logs there are here!"

Dinga (N): beef.

Dingabledinga (S): water everywhere.

Dingo (Q): the wild dog. It was also tamed and used in hunting, and was probably brought to Australia thousands of years ago. The original tribal name was possibly *jungho*. *Dingo* was used and applied also to places in New South Wales.

Dirigeree (N): willy wagtail.

Dirkah (Q): smoke.

Ditta Ditta (N): spurwing plover.

Dobikin (N): a small watercourse.

Donarah (N): ribs.

Donnabewong (V): ashes like sawdust.

Doogumburrum (Q): honeycomb. Now Rocky Point.

Dookenine (W): roasting.

Doolanghooterghu (N): a man becoming agitated when crossing a bog, feeling his way with a stick, and suddenly finding that it is disappearing in the soft mud.

Dooloo (N): a spear.

Doongorwah (N): a rock with water running over it.

Doradeen (W): a little rock hole.

Dorrigo (N): stringy bark tree.

Dougalook (V): a wattle bird or honeysucker.

Dougan (N): a high mountain.

Dourim (N): a crossing place. Now South Arm.

Dowarran (W): bayonet-bill parrot.

Dowcan (N): land; to walk.

Dowgimbee (N): a mussel ground.

Dreelwarrina (N): a reed standing up. Several New South Wales names incorporate the root word *dreel*.

Drucwalla (N): plenty of water. The name was applied to a beautiful creek in the Jamberoo Mountain.

Dubbo (N): from *thubbo* or *tubbo*, a name for a cap or head covering. The material of which it is made is in dispute. Some say that it was of possum fur, others that it was a headband, and others that *tubbo* was the skin of the breast of an eagle hawk with the feathers plucked but the down still adhering, and made into a skull cap. Again, *dubbo* is the white clay from which a head covering was made. If this is so, then the headgear would be a mourning cap worn by widows after their husband's death.

Duckan Duckan (N): grey gum tree. Now Ramornie.

Duelgum (N): a large eel. Now Solferino.

Dugalup (W): a gully with a running stream.

Dugandan (Q): a type of reed suitable for making dilly bags, growing beside a spring on the hillside.

Duggie (Q): a knife.

Dulcoon (N): to be injured; to become sick.

Dulcoonghi (N): a place of sickness.

Dulcoonghihy or **Dulcoonghiny** (N): a place where sick people were removed to.

Dulgambone (N): dry, hard earth. Also known as Deepwater.

Dulgum (N): a big flood.

Dullungil (N): pipeclay.

Dum (N): yams.

Dumbermanning (W): the pouch of a kangaroo.

Dumbleyung (W): place where a game called *dumbung* was played.

Dumbulli (N): a place for a dance.

Dumbum (N): a place where *dum* (yams) were plentiful. Now Nettle Creek.

Dumpaal (Q): road, path, track.

Dunbible (N): from *tunbible*, a tree.

Dundeppa (Q): a look-out. Now Garden Island.

Dundilkar (N): the gum of the cabbage tree palm. Now Double Swamp.

Dundullimal (N): from *dundullamahl* or *thunthullimal*, which have been translated as the work of a hailstorm; a terrific hailstorm; or the place of large hailstones.

Dundundra (N): a rapid or waterfall.

Dunedoo (N): a swan.

Dungarubba (N): an open plain; a swamp.

Dungate (N): a goanna. Now Dengate.

Dungatewakaah (N): from *dungate*, a goanna; *wakaah*, a creek. Goanna Creek.

Dungay (N): thin sheets of bark from the white gum tree.

Dungog (N): from *tunkok*, bare or clear hill.

Dungullin (W): permanent water.

Dunnangmumma (N): to catch a man by the heel.

Dunoon (N): a ridge.

Dunowie (N): reply to little ant.

Dunwinnie (Q): an emu.

Durakai (Q): dense scrub.

Dural (N): hollow tree on fire; smoking hollow tree.

Duri (N): to crawl; a snake crawling in the grass.

Durra (N): see *Darra*.

Durradulee (N): a waterfall.

Durranbah (N): a jumper ant.

Durran Durran (N): dry ground.

Durrebar (W): a black cockatoo.

Durrumbi or **Turrumbi** (N): a stake.

Dwella (Q): father.

Dyrarba (N): sandhills.

Dyum (Q): summer.

E

Eabrai (N): a mountain close by. Now Wellingrove.

Eabungyalgo (N): drought.

Earamboo (N): small smoke.

Earea Dam (S): native bush.

Earin (N): a whip snake.

Earindi (N): a hill without trees. Now Furracabad.

Echuca (V): meeting of the waters; junction of the rivers. Earlier Aboriginal names were *whungulingia* and *woolithiga*, and it is possible that *echuca* is a corruption of *ithiga*, the local tribal name. Echuca was decided upon by the early surveyors from the local Aborigines' description of themselves.

Echunga (S): close.

Edgeroi (N): a creek.

Edibegebege (W): plenty of fleas.

Edieowie (S): from *ethie*, diamond sparrow; *owie*, water.

Edillilie (S): two springs close together.

Enaweena (N): a woman by the fire.

Eenerweena (N): a little woman.

Einbunpin (Q): from *yinbunban*, an edible root.

Ejuncum (Q): grassy; long grass.

Elanora (Q): a camp by the sea.

Ellengerah (N): from *nulloin*, pebble; *dheran*, eating. A man eating white pebbles.

Ellingerah (N): wind and water. From *gerah*, wind; *colleen*, water.

Elouera (N): pleasant place; a good camping ground by the seashore. The site was selected because plenty of food was available at this place.

Eneby (Q): the name of the local tribe.

Enoggera (Q): from *ynoggera*.

Epuldugger (Q): a haunted spot avoided by people. There was a belief amongst many tribes that after death the spirit of the deceased remained behind and became a malevolent ghost or evil spirit. For this reason camps were abandoned and not revisited for many years until the memory of the death had been forgotten.

Eragorara (N): white ant; a camp recently abandoned.

Eringanerin (N): from *eringanerong*, wood duck.

Ermara (Q): where it is always raining.

Ettamogah (N): to have a drink; let's have a drink.

Euchareena (N): named after an Aboriginal.

Euchie (N): a dingo.

Eudunda (S): named after a nearby spring which was called *Eudundacowie*.

Eulah Creek and Mountain (Q): named after an Aboriginal who accompanied the Jardines on their expedition in 1864.

Eulomogo (N): without finger nails.

Eumminbung (N): good luck.

Eumungerie (N): a tree.

Eungai (N): singing creek.

Eungella (Q): mountain of the mists.

Eurabuga (N): a dead, maggoty emu; stinking camp.

Euraman (N): a horse; literally, something with two large front teeth, which was feared as a supernatural monster.

Eurie Eurie (N): parrots.

Euro- (N): a prefix widely used in New South Wales, meaning sun.

Euroa (V): from *yerao*, joyful, happy.

Eurobodalla (N): from *urobodalla*, a small haven for canoes; land between the waters.

Euroka (N): sun; sunlit corner.

Eurunderee (N): a lone tree. Henry Lawson's parents erected their tent under a blue gum which gave its name to the district.

Ewingar (N): a small shrub or tree.

Ewmbunlie (N): a child crying.

Eyerah (Q): a lancewood tree (notable for its straight wood which was useful for making spears).

F

Ferritcartup (W): plenty of silver wattle.

G

Gab- (W): a prefix which enters many Western Australian names, meaning water.

Gabagong or **Gabeegong** (W): fresh water close to the sea.

Gabakile (W): water in the bend. Now Esperance.

Gabelbuttering (W): a spring in the forest.

Gaberline (W): a good water hole.

Gabyellia (W): a gully with a stream.

Gabyon (W): water close to the surface.

Gadara (N): cold; windy; to feel a draught.

Gailagup (W): devil's hill.

Galantapa (V): a place where a tree was cut down.

Galga (S): hungry.

Galgopin (W): a place where two big fires were made.

Galliebarinda (N): a waterfall or cascade.

Galong (N): a swampy plain; flying fox.

Gammain (N): cooked.

Gangalook (N): echo. The name was given to the mountain.

Ganibup (W): a running spring.

Ganmain (N): a man decorated with scars. These were usually a sign of manhood or womanhood. Gashes were made with sharp stone knives or shells, and a mixture of fat and ashes rubbed into the wounds. They acted as a healing agent, and helped to raise the scars, which were greatly admired.

Garah (N): far off; distant.

Garema (N): a camp.

Garie (N): see *Geera*.

Garoolgan (N): a single man going to a fight.

Garradarrow (N): stones. The station which was later established here was named Stoney Station.

Garrapun (N): hailstones.

Garriguronga (N): quicksand country.

Gathong (Q): a little girl.

Gayndah (Q): from *gainda* or *giunda*, thunder; or from *ngainta*, scrubby country.

Gearywah (N): a goanna. Now Black Head.

Geearangrib (N): white gum tree with the bark lifted from the butt; white scrub. Now called Acacia Creek.

Geelong (V): a swampy plain.

Geera, Garie, or **Geara** (N): In spite of its appearance this is not an Aboriginal name. It is said to be named after a bushranger named Geary who camped here.

Geeringgeerindah (N): the place of grey hairs.

Geerydjine (N): a stinging tree.

Geerymbeerindal (N): tadpoles.

Geetchboordankendoo (W): spears broken up.

Gemalla (N): fish.

Genanaguy (N): get on with what you are doing.

Gerongar (N): a place where the *gerongar* grows. It is a root which has medicinal properties.

Gerringong (N): fearful; I fear myself. It was at this point that the Aborigines first saw the sails of Cook's *Endeavour* out at sea and expressed their fear. See also *Jerrungarugh*.

Gerrut (Q): a good place for a camp.

Getten (N): moon. Now Long Reach.

Gheera (N): a wild turkey. Now Mount Keira.

Gibba (Q): camp here tonight.

Gibber (N): a hollow rock. *Gibber* is the name for rock or stone. See names that follow in this list.

Gibberagee (N): the pepper-mint tree, which grows main-ly on poor rocky country.

Gibberagong (N): plenty of rocks.

Gibberagunyah or **Gibbergunyah** (N): literally a stone hut, but is used for a cave or rock shelter used for human ac-commodation.

Gibboke (V): a sharp thorn which pierced the feet of the Aborigines at this place.

Gibingbell (Q): a wild orange tree.

Gidgaween or **Gidgerwean** (N): burnt grass.

Gigidin (W): a small round pool.

Gigil (W): a sparrow hawk.

Gilba (W): grass.

Gilgai (W): a little hole sur-rounded by grass.

Gilgandra (N): from *carlginda*, *carlgindra*, or *kalagandra*, a long water hole. Named for the large natural water hole in the Castlereagh River at this place.

Gil Gil Bore (N): literally flowing away, running away from. The creek overflowed its banks but after flowing for several miles returned again to the creek.

Gilgoenbone (N): place of bloody ribs.

Gilla (Q): the wild hop.

Gillamagong (N): house of the big white man. "Big" in this case means rich.

Gillawarna (N): from *gillah-wurna*, the galah bird.

Gillebri (N): moonshine.

Gillendoon (N): from *killen-doon*, to turn back a crowd of people.

Gillimanning (W): poison.

Gillingkeleen (N): fishing lines.

Gilyne (W): a dove hawk.

Gimboolam (N): a long range of high mountains.

Ginairrunda (Q): a frilled lizard.

Gineroi (N): from *gheewari*, place of the logs; dead trees about.

Gingham (N): from *gheenham*, between; in the middle; in the heart of.

Gingie (N): foam; froth on the water.

Gingilin (N): a barren moun-tain.

Gin Gin (Q): from *jinjinburra*, the name of the local tribe.

Gin Gin (N): moss.

Giree Giree (N): a river with high banks. Now Inverell.

Girilambone (N): from *ghirra-langbone*, place of many stars; place where a star fell. It is interesting to note a report that flint stones were procured here, reputed to have come from a meteor.

Giro (N): a black satin bird.

Girral (N): grey box trees.

Girraween (N): place of flowers.

Gkoonwarra (N): a high point of land with smooth, round stones. Now Koonawarra.

Gnahrool (N): a place partly surrounded by water.

Gnaroo (N): honey.

Gnarriatta (N): a shell.

Gnijong (N): that fellow! (A contemptuous expression.) Now Nijong.

Gnullum (V): a reed used by the Aborigines to suck water out of the ground.

Gnurrlarkendockenerup (W): a man jumped on and his ribs broken.

Goanah (Q): plenty of grass.

Gobblin (W): spring running through the rocks.

Goblebackinglup (W): belly of the hill. This is a creek which runs at the foot of Mount Barker.

Gobung (Q): dead; died.

Gogeldrie (N): a canoe made from a hollow tree.

Gol Gol (N): a good place for a meeting.

Goline (W): good shelter.

Gongeway (N): many shells scattered over the beach.

Gongora (Q): a crocodile in the lagoon.

Gooallie (N): ugly.

Goodah (N): dark.

Goodalup (W): wallaby thicket.

Goodawada (N): laughing jack-ass.

Goodawadda (N): good timber for making spears.

Goodie Goodie (Q): plenty of birds.

Goodooga (N): a big lagoon; a yam.

Googean (N): a sugar ant.

Googee (N): a hunting ground for kangaroos and possums.

Goola (N): a kangaroo.

Goolahgelum (N): a fighting ground.

Goolamera (N): drooping trees.

Goolarabang (N): blackbutt trees.

Goolengdoogee (N): split fore-head.

Gooloorooeybri (N): bullfrogs.

Goolwa (S): the elbow.

Goomagully (Q): a wattle tree.

Goombaban (N): dusty soil.

Goompie (Q): round like a ball. Now Dunwich.

Goonal (N): a big lagoon.

Goonambil (N): a place covered with human excrement.

Goonambong (N): a part of the bora or initiation ground.

Goonaring (W): a stinking spring.

Goonaroo (N): a wood duck.

Goondam (N): rain; storm.

Goonderin (W): a place where a man had a bad leg.

Goondi (N): a camp; stringy-bark timber country; bark dents; over there; far away.

Goondiwindi (Q and N): a place where wild ducks are found; water running over rocks;

while another explanation is that the two words *goona* and *winnah* refer to the droppings of ducks or shags, and that many of these birds resting on a rock caused it to become white.

Goondooloo (S): the constellation of the Southern Cross.

Goondorrabrolga (N): a native companion.

Goonegah (N): a large clear space where corroborees are held.

Goonellabah (N): native coral tree.

Goong (N): a storm.

Goonian (N): a child born here.

Goongiwarri (N): a swamp.

Goongoora (N): yellow stone used for tattooing. This is the rendering given by one authority, but probably all that is implied is that the yellow ochre was used in body painting.

Gooninbah or **Gooningbah** (N): place of the *gooning* or porcupine.

Goonong (N): native mignonette, a plant with a disagreeable smell. Also *Goononbil*.

Goonoo (N): blind man; one-eyed man; anything that has been planted, as distinct from growing wild.

Goonoo Goonoo (N): from *goon*, water; *o*, with. The name therefore has been translated

plenty of water; place of good water; other explanations are: poor country for game; coughing.

Goonoonggeereby (N): a magpie.

Goora (N): a component of many place names in New South Wales. Alternative forms are *goora*, *gooram*, *goori*, *goorah*. The essential meaning is long or tall. Examples in the names that follow are Goorabil, Goorabin. Goorah, Gooraway, Goorari, Gooraman, Gooradool, Gooradjin. There were many other names which have now been lost.

Gooraanghee (N): a round hill.

Gooraanghi (N): red pigment.

Goorabil (N): place of the tall pine trees.

Goorabin (N): a long swamp.

Goorack Goorack (M): a camp in the hills.

Gooradjin (N): a long or high-peaked hill; a long or high point. Now Gragin.

Gooradool (N): a tall man.

Gooragoodoo (N): small grey doves.

Goorah (N): a long swamp.

Gooraman (N): a long sheet of water; a long grassy glade.

Gooramma (N): glade; a long glade.

Goorari (N): a place of tall pine trees.

Goorawan (N): large stones in the water.

Gooraway (N): to go round; big, or high rocks.

Goorawigah (N): a fishing place.

Goorawin (N): flowers.

Gooray (Q): this word has some connection with a cypress pine ridge near the present railway line.

Gooringaragunambone (N): hair growing out of the ears.

Gooro (N): a big gorge.

Gootering (Q): a rosella parrot.

Gootoo (N): bad.

Gooulloah (Q): a porpoise.

Gooung (N): smoky. Now Smoky Cape.

Gorimu (Q): spinifex.

Gorrah (Q): plenty of possums.

Gorrijup (W): a palm swamp.

Gorung (N): where the river runs into the sea.

Goudjoulgang (N): camp. Now Rose Bay.

Goullan (W): a place where a woman was killed.

Gourwin (N): a water hole.

Gowayoo (N): wait a bit.

Gowrie (N): down of an eagle hawk. This was eagerly sought and prized because of its use when decorating the body for various ceremonies.

Goyda (S): possibly from *guida*, a river with red banks.

Graman (N): from *gooraman*, big plain; long plain; glade.

Grong Grong (N): a poor camping ground; very hot.

Grooman (Q): a kangaroo's tail.

Groombunda (N): bloodwood trees.

Groongal (N): from *koroongal*, long grass.

Gruegarnie (N): stinging fish. Now Burie Creek.

Guaballing (W): plenty of red earth.

Guabothoo (N): see *Quabothoo*.

Guagong (N): from *cugong*, place where the river overflows.

Guean (N): a possum.

Guerie (N): a white cockatoo.

Gugetup (W): kangaroo dung flat.

Guine (Q): an arm.

Gular (N): from *gulargambone*, plenty of galah birds.

Gulargambone (N): see *Gular* above.

Gulark (W): a bird known as squeaker.

Gulgong (N): a deep water hole.

Gulgorah (N): a bird known as a leatherhead.

Gullallie (N): a ravine.

Gulligal (N): long grass seed.

Gullingari (N): to fall from a height.

Gullingoorun (N): a long water hole.

Gumbowie (S): a name which has some connection with water.

Gumeracha (S): from *umeracha*.

Gumma Gumma (N): plenty of pipeclay.

Gummin Gummin (N): to parry a spear by means of a shield.

Gunaga (N): a group of water holes.

Gundagai (N): from *gunda-bandobingee*, to cut the back of the knee with a tomahawk. Other meanings: sinews; going upstream.

Gundaroo (N): a big water hole.

Gundeerari (N): feathers of a bird.

Gundemain or **Gundimaian** (N): from *gundimyan*, house by a stream.

Gunderlong (N): a place where many mahogany trees are growing.

Gunderman (N): a horse.

Gundi (N): stringybark tree; over there; far away; bark huts.

Gundimaian (N): see *Gundemain*.

Gundurimbah (N): from *coondoorimbah*, a man with bad eyes.

Gundy (N): from *goondhi*, a stringybark tree. See also *Gundi*. Now Arthurville.

Gungalla (N): rushes.

Gunggari (W): to sit down.

Gunida (N): see *Gunnedah*.

Guniwaraldi (N): limestone or white stones scattered over the ground, from *guni*, white stones.

Gunnamatta (N): beach and sandhills. See *Cronulla*.

Gunnedah or **Gunida** (N): from *guni*, a white stone. The locality was noted for its barren stoniness, and the name has therefore been translated: many white stones; place of white stones; place of destitution.

Gunning (N): from *goonong*, swamp mahogany; or from *gunnrang*, small water courses.

Guntawang (N): meeting place.

Gunyah (N): shelter; hut; house. A *gunyah* was a quickly built hut of branches interwoven with brush, which afforded good shelter in bad weather.

Gunyan (N): a place where a child died.

Gunyerwarildi (N): a large creek.

Guoingon (N): stars.

Gurana (Q): bees.

Gurin Gurin (N): white stones.

Gurley (N): a creek.

Guroura (N): a place frequented by possums. Now Kurrara.

Gurrai (S): refreshments; food.

Gurranong (N): sugar.

Gurregory (N): a river with high banks.

Gurri (N): a stout woman.

Gutchboordankendockenarup (W): spears broken up.

Guyra (N): fish can be caught; fishing place; white cockatoo.

Gwydir or **Gwyder** (N): a river with red banks.

Gygam (N): a cut foot.

Gymea Bay (N): a giant lily; a small bird.

Gympie (Q): from *gympi gympi*, a stinging tree. These trees were believed to be a protection against evil spirits. Formerly Nashville.

H

Harah (Q): the sky.

Hennendri (N): from *inariendri*. *Ina* was a woman. It was the place where Aboriginal women were sold or bartered for blankets, implements, etc.

Hillamah (N): a small shield.

Hinnomunjie (V): codfish.

Holpin (N): forest oaks. Now Stonehenge.

Honka (Q): a tiger snake.

Hookina (S): a shrub with long, edible roots.

Horrowill (N): plenty of gum trees. Now Marowon.

Howlong (Q): plenty of fish.

Howregan (W): a place where wild hens laid their eggs.

I

Iarangutta (Q): plenty of crocodiles.

Iargarong (Q): plenty of flying foxes.

Iarranguatta (Q): where the tide comes in.

Ichemen (Q): plenty of water wagtails.

Iggin (N): a cold place.

Illabo (N): a curious explanation for this name. It is said that it was first called *Billabong*, but that as there were so many places with this name, it was changed to *illabo* by removing the letters b, n, and g from the original name. A direct translation has been given as: where.

Illabunda (N): swallows.

Illalong (N): swampy plain; a resort for native companions.

Illawambra (N): from *ullawamburragh*, a dwarf tree.

Illawarra (N): There are several explanations of this name. *Elouera*, a pleasant place by the sea. From *illa*, white clay, *warra*, a hill, hence the version white clay hill. Again, as *wurra* or *warra* meant a high place or mountain in the language spoken by the Aborigines between Woolongong and Shoalhaven, it has been rendered either a mountain, or a high place near the sea. See also *Illowra*.

Illbonden (Q): many water holes.

Illilliwa (N): the setting sun.
Illowra (N): a beautiful place; place of plenty; white fish eagle.
Illpah (N): plenty of raspberries. Now Waterloo.
Iloura (N): lake, or calm water (in contrast to the storminess of the ocean).
Iluka (N): near the sea.
-in, -ine, and **-ing** (W): common place name terminations, especially in Western Australia.
Inderwong (W): a bright star.
Indi (N): something far away, or belonging to the distant past. It was the Aboriginal name for the source of the Murray River and the surrounding country. It may possibly have been a contraction of *goondiwiindi*, meaning a bark hut made a long time ago.
Indiamba (N): smooth, glossy.
Indooroopilly (Q): a gully of leeches.
Ingar (N): from *ingah*, crayfish.
Ingenup (W): a blackboy thicket surrounded by hills.
Ingildo (N): very bad.
Inglegar (N): from *inglegar*, a place of sick people.
Ingra (W): the burrows of native rats.
Innamincka (S): from *yidni-minkani*, meaning you pass into hole, or you go into the

hole there. The name comes from an old legend in which a totemic ancestor commanded a rainbow snake to go into the hole. The town was at one time known as Hopetoun, but later changed to the original name.
Irkara (Q): plenty of eggs.
Ironmongie (N): a large white ant.
Ivanjah (Q): an old woman.

J

Jabbarup (W): plenty of grass.
Jabuk (S): Aboriginal word for bullock.
Jackey Jackey Creek and Range (Q): named for the Aboriginal boy who was a survivor of the Kennedy expedition.
Jakabulga (N): a waterfall.
Jamberoo (N): from *jambaroo*, a track.
Jannali (N): moon.
Japergiling (W): a marrying place.
Jarara (N): a rock with water flowing over it.
Jarramarumba (Q): this place is good.
Jebropilly (Q): flying squirrel gully.
Jeedbowlee (N): a place where a headman prayed for fine weather. No doubt the headman was a wirinun or rainmaker on whose skill the

tribe depended to ensure that they had sufficient rainfall.

Jeeljarrup (W): three jarrah trees grown together.

Jeggibil (Q): plenty of green birds always here.

Jelleejuddo (N): a place where pipis were first made by the god or spirit Beeroogoon.

Jembyrinjah (N): a Blue Mountain parrot.

Jennacubine (W): salt and fresh water pools lying close together.

Jenolan Caves (N): the origin of the name is uncertain. The Aborigines called the locality *Binoomea*, while at a little distance is a mountain called *Genowlan*. The name was probably conferred by a European, and one amusing theory is that it was in honour of J. Nolan, an early settler. The only literal meaning we have seen advanced is: foot.

Jenymungup (W): plenty of gum.

Jerbam (N): grubs used for bait.

Jercruba (Q): full of shells.

Jerendine (W): a big hullo.

Jerilderie (M): possibly from *jereeldrie*, a place of reeds. There is an apochryphal story that the wife of an early settler called her husband "Gerald dearie", and so the settlement got its name.

Jerrabung (N): an old man.

Jerrara (N): a place where eels sleep, or lie down.

Jerrawa (N): goanna.

Jerrungarugh (N): ambush, a name commemorating a tribal fight. Now Gerringong.

Jerry Jerry (V): a spurwing plover.

Jerula (N): a reed spear. Light toy spears were often made for boys to give them practice in spear throwing. The larger reed spear could be used for fishing and even for hunting.

Jiggi (N): from *jiguary*, the cat bird, or the call of the cat bird. Also a reed which grew in the swamps near Lismore.

Jiggijah (N): a place where the *jiggi* reed grows.

Jilderie (V): a reedy place.

Jillamatong (N): a large isolated mountain.

Jillamunna (N): a small isolated mountain.

Jimmicubine (N): running water.

Jindabyne (N): a valley.

Jindalee (N): a bare hill; no skin on the bones.

Jingara (N): a large mountain believed to be inhabited by a *yaramayhawho*, a fabulous creature with a cavernous mouth, which preyed on unsuspecting tribesmen and women.

Jingerah (N): a steep mountain with precipitous sides, difficult to climb.

Jingubullaworrigee (N): will go there; it is not far.

Jinna (Q): the foot.

Jinnerbeeker (W): bad feet.

Jinnerculurdy (W): big feet.

Jinnetberrin (W): a small bird and a nearby forest.

Joalah (N): a place of pheasants.

Jooriland (N): rocks and water holes.

Jubuck (W): a native potato.

Jukemering (W): thigh bones of kangaroos.

Julago (Q): a plain turkey.

Jular (N): a native bear. Now Bungwall Flat.

Jumberdine (W): a large camp.

Jumbullah (N): plenty of wild game about. Now Mount Kembla.

Jumpinpin (Q): root or sucker of the pandanus tree, used for chewing.

Junburra (N): flies. Now Appletree Flat.

Jundah (Q): a woman.

Junee (N): possibly from *chunee*, frog; or, speak to me.

Jungay (Q): the west wind.

Junnearupy (W): a split rock.

Junynnmgup (W): plenty of gum.

Jurinpudding (W): many rugged hills.

K

Kadina (S): from *caddyyeena* or *kaddyinna*, lizard plain.

Kadlunga (S): from *kadla*, sweet. At one time there was a great deal of honeysuckle in this area.

Kadungle (N): a small lizard.

Kaghil (N): bad, bitter water.

Kahibah (N): from *kaibur*, active; eager.

Kairaraba (N): from *kaiara*, seaweed; place of seaweed.

Kalachalpa (S): creek of plenty. Now Anna Creek.

Kalangadoo (S): from *kalangbool*, a swamp with many red gum trees.

Kalbar (Q): a star. Formerly Engelsburg.

Kalgoorlie (W): possibly from *calgoola* or *kalgurli*, three parallel tracks, or three lines in the shape of a fork.

Kalgoorliegunyah (W): water from trees at the meeting of the tracks.

Kalguddering (W): a clump of rushes.

Kallatene (N): see *Kullateenee*.

Kallaroo (W): cold weather.

Kallgallup (W): a camp fire.

Kallibucca (N): bent tallow wood trees.

Kallioota (S): evergreen.

Kallulahwon (W): a big bush fire.

Kalpara (Q): the dry sandy bed of a river.

Kalyan (S): you stay here; wait.

Kalybucca (N): from *kaly*, water; *bucca*, crooked: crooked creek.

Kalyra (S): the name of a timber from which spears were made. Also called Avenue Range.

Kamarah (N): sleep.

Kamarga (Q): a storm.

Kamber (N): a spring.

Kameruka (N): wait here till I come; wait here till I come back.

Kamo (Q): plain of water (lake).

Kanaipa (Q): ironbark spear.

Kanandah (N): the land where the sun sets.

Kangaloola or **Kanglooa** (N): kangaroo hunting ground.

Kangarilla (S): from *kangooa-rinilla*, a place where the mother sheep sits down. It was once owned by Eyre and known as Eyre's Flat.

Kangiangi (N): from *kangi*, mangrove: a creek with mangroves growing in it.

Kangowirranilla (S): a place for kangaroos and water. Now Macclesfield.

Kanimbla (N): big fight; fighting ground.

Kanni (S): a frilled lizard.

Kanowna (W): named after a boy who died at this place.

Kapunda (S): from *cappieoonda*, water jumping out or pos-sibly place of smoke.

Karaak Flat (N): spittle.

Karakanba (N): a place of swamp oaks.

Karangi (N): a duck.

Kareelah (N): the south wind.

Kareelpa (Q): plenty of rats.

Kargon (Q): large kingfishers.

Karkoo (S): a she-oak.

Karkuburra (Q): a laughing jackass.

Karoonda (S): a winter camp.

Karrara (Q): plenty of pebbles on the beach.

Karratha (W): hard-bottomed.

Karrawirraparri (S): a river of red gum forest. Now Torrens River.

Karte (S): low, thick scrub.

Karuah (N): a native plum tree.

Katanning (W): from *kartannin*, chief meeting place.

Katoomba (N): from *katta-toonbah*, waters tumble over hill; or from *kadumba* or *kudumba*, falling water, or falling together of many streams.

Kawana (Q): flowers.

Kechualing (W): many spears made here.

Keechipup (W): a good thicket of trees known as *woorie-mongron*, from which the best spears were made.

Keeden (N): the moon.

Keedirah (N): after a bush fire.

Keelbubban (N): sound of rippling water.

Keelkeelba (N): a place of grass trees.

Keera (N): a big lagoon.

Keerang (V): the moon.

Keewong (N): where the moon camped.

Keira, Mount (N): from *keera*, wild turkey; high mountain.

Keirbarban (N): a white ants' nest. Now Broadwater.

Kelpum (Q): a large mountain.

Kembla, Port (N): abundant game; plenty of wild fowl.

Kerrabee (N): from *corroboree*, the occasion of light-hearted dances, games, and songs, sometimes as a prelude to the initiation ceremonies.

Kerrick (Q): a white cockatoo.

Kewol (Q): deep water.

Kiacatoo (N): wooden shovel.

Kiah (N): a beautiful place.

Kiaka (W): a place of many hills.

Kiama (N): possibly from *Kiahma*, an alternative form of Baiame (there are many spellings), the famous father spirit of eastern New South Wales. See *Byamee*. Or from *kiaremia* or *kiaramia*, fish caught from the rocks; good fishing ground; plenty of food.

Kiandool (N): a baby.

Kiandra (N): sharp stones used as knives.

Kianee (N): a big mussel. Now Batten's Bight.

Kianga (N): to fish with a light. Fish were caught in streams and lagoons by means of light spears from canoes, and attracted by torchlight.

Kiara (N): a white cockatoo.

Kiavolo (Q): a goose.

Kieinde (N): a bathing place.

Kielpa (S): a short distance; near.

Kiemai (N): a swimming hole.

Kihi (N): fond of women.

Kijini (N): a playground or place where corroborees are held.

Kiki (S): a water hole; also for worms obtained in the vicinity.

Killara (N): always there.

Killawarra (N): scrub; in the scrub.

Killerberrin (W): an old water hole.

Killie (N): a night owl.

Killiting (W): springs running dry.

Killanoola (S): a black jay's nest.

Killowill (N): a black duck.

Killumboolth (V): named after the headman of the local tribe. Now Bessiebelle.

Kilto (S): grassy.

Kimba (S): fire in the bush.

Kincumber (N): belonging to the old man.

Kindaitchin (N): plenty of stones. Now Glen Innes.

Kindee (N): chips cut from a log.

Kindilan (Q): jolly; happy.

Kingaroy (Q): possibly from *kinjerroy*, red ant.

Kingimbon (N): rocks.

Kingurra (Q): a black swan.

Kinka (Q): a night owl.

Kinnibill (N): a swan.

Kinninggere (N): oysters.

Kiparra (N): the place where the *kiparra* ceremony was performed. This was a local name for the initiation ceremonies at which boys were admitted to full manhood.

Kirip (S): a boxwood tree.

Kittani (N): a big mountain covered with scrub.

Kiwa (N): daylight.

Kiwarrick (N): a lump on a tree. It seems likely that this would be the excrescence on a tree trunk which was cut off and used to make a coolamon.

Kiyung (N): a long sandy beach.

Knamerilup (W): a great place for ferns.

Knonghetup (W): the call of the swan.

Knooticup (W): many red gum trees. In this variety the gum trickled down the bark like a stream of blood.

Knulgoweedie (W): a corroboree ground.

Kogarah (N): from *koggerah* or *coogoorah*, a place where the rushes grow; a reedy swamp. Now Rushcutters Bay.

Kogoor (Q): a porcupine.

Koichgomorlgup (W): a place where there are flints for making axe heads. They are chipped to give them a sharp edge and affixed to wooden handles by means of gum or the sinews of animals.

Koikalingba (N): from *koikaling*, a bramble with a berry resembling a raspberry. The full name means a place of brambles.

Kollien (N): from *kolli*, water; *en*, cloudy or white; cloudy or white water.

Kollimungool (N): from *kollie*, water; *mungool*, white, or spreading: broad or spreading water.

Kolodong (N): a dove.

Koloona (N): a young man.

Kolorinbri (N): many *kolorin* — the flowers of the *kurubah* tree.

Kolyourgouring (W): a big spring.

Konakonabe or **Konakonaba** (N): This is a mountain to the north of Lake Macquarie where the *konakona* is found. It is a yellow substance contained in veins of the stone from which paint is made for body decoration in preparation for fighting expeditions.

Kondoparinga (S): a long winding waterway between steep banks where crayfish are found in abundance. The name was given by Governor Robe.

Kongoola (Q): a mountain.

Kongorong (S): a corruption of *koongeronoong*, the corner.

Kononda (S): northwards.

Kooelung (N): a porpoise. The porpoises could often be seen from this place.

Koolamurranaila (N): big goanna walk about.

Koolanjin (N): forked sticks in the ground.

Koolatai (N): from *kooloo*, seed; *tai*, the end of, or this side of: this side where plenty of seed grows.

Koolbung (W): a saltwater swamp.

Koolewong (N): a native bear.

Koolilabah (N): a water lily.

Kooloobong (N): from *kooloo*, seeds; *bong*, a creek or lagoon: seeds beside a creek or watercourse.

Koolunga (S): red banks. This place on the Broughton River was at one time known as Hope's Crossing.

Koolywurtie (S): a rugged, rocky point jutting into the sea.

Koomooloo (S): it has been said that this name has no particular meaning but it was coined by Thomas Warnes, an early landowner.

Koona (N): a place where the *koona*, the root of which has medicinal properties, grows.

Koona (Q): a yam.

Koonadan (N): a canoe.

Koonawarra (N): see *Gkoonwarra*.

Koongburry (N): seaweed floating on top of the water.

Koonging (V): named after the headman of the local tribe. Now Dartmor.

Koongool (Q): honey.

Koonthaparee (Q): a place where men die.

Kooparaback (N): a saltwater creek.

Koora (S): abundance; plenty.

Kooraegulla (N): good morning, brother (a greeting).

Koorakooraby (W): spring of the bearded snake.

Koorarawlyee (W): a large tree stump holding water.

Koorawatha (N): place of pine trees.

Kooreelah, see *Carra Carra*.

Koorine (S): my daughter.

Kooringa (S): a she-oak and water.

Kooroomie (N): a woman's breasts. Now Horse Bend.

Kooroora (Q): a camp.

Kootapatamba (N): a water hole where eagles drink, on top of a mountain.

Kootingal (N): a star.

Kooweerup (V): blackfish swimming.

Kooyalee (Q): spear grass.

Kopperamanna (S): from *kaparamara*, a root shaped like a hand.

Koppio (S): oysters.

Kopurraba (N): from *koparra*, a kind of earth which was moistened, rolled into a ball, and roasted in a hot fire, when it turned a brilliant red in colour. When ground and mixed with fat it was used for body painting.

Korewal (N): a strong person. Now La Perouse.

Koriminnup (W): plenty of hazel nuts.

Koro (Q): eye.

Korogaro (N): many barnacles clinging to the rocks.

Korogoro, Cape (N): a place with three headlands.

Koroit (V): a fire.

Kotara (N): a club or waddy.

Koulabelamba (N): where the eagles drink.

Kouming (N): scum on the eye.

Kououk (N): a crane.

Krambakh (N): a kind of gum tree. The bark of this tree was used for making torches.

Kringen (S): to spring up.

Krowathunkoolung (V): the country belonging to the men from the east. Now Croajenalong.

Kuac (W): tobacco.

Kubura (N): a young man attending an initiation ceremony.

Kudgeree (N): raw flesh. Later Cudgera Head. Now Point Hastings.

Kulde (S): brothers.

Kulgoa (N): returning; running through.

Kulguddering (W): a clump of rushes.

Kulgun (Q): a good path; a clear track. Formerly called Schneider's Road.

Kullaroo (W): a road leading to water.

Kullateenee, Kullatine, or **Kallateene** (N): a place where the grass has often been burned. It was the custom of hunters to set fire to the grass on a plain in order to drive the game towards them. This process enriched the soil and encouraged the growth of many plants.

Kulpara (S): water in head.

Kulwararabooka (N): a place of quandong trees.

Kumal (N): a place where a man died.

Kunama (N): snow.

Kunanty (Q): an emu.

Kundabung (N): a place where wild apples grow.

Kundle Kundle (N): from *kundul*, the wild carrot. Cundletown was a name which was derived from this word. Another place where the wild carrot was plentiful was on the southern shore of Botany Bay where Captain Cook made his landing.

Kundul (N): see *Kundle Kundle*.

Kungala (N): to shout.

Kungaree (Q): a knife.

Kunghah (N): to collect or gather together. The name was given by local Aborigines after they had collected strayed cattle and brought them to this place.

Kunjara (Q): a dry time; drought.

Kunjavurra (Q): a black shag.

Kunlara (S): a native companion.

Kuorigoora (N): a vine which was used in climbing trees.

Kuranda (Q): a plant.

Kurdnatta (S): a place of drifting sand. Now Port Augusta.

Kuringai (N): the name of the tribes which inhabited the coastal district.

Kurnalpi (W): a clear sky.

Kurnel (N): from *kundul*, the wild carrot. This is the place referred to as Cook's landing place. See *Kundle Kundle*.

Kurrajong (N): the tree which was as useful to the Aborigines as it is to pastoralists of a later age. It provided shade; the strong bark was used for many purposes, especially for making cord for fishing nets and lines, and dilly bags; while the roots provided food. There are many variants of the name: currajong, currijong, koorajong, etc.

Kurrawah (M): a stingray.

Kurrawonga (N): a bustard turkey.

Kurri Kurri (N): man; ear; the very first.

Kurumbul (Q): a scrub magpie.

Kuttai (N): a peninsula.

Kwinana (W): a young woman.

Kyarran (N): a frog.

Kybybolite (S): a runaway hole; a place where ghosts are found.

Kynnumboon (Q): a place of possums.

Kyogle (N): a plain turkey; a native companion.

Kywung or **Kywong** (N): a camping place; a resting place.

L

Lalaguli (Q): a water-nymph.

Langaur (Q): sleep.

Laragon (Q): married.

Larow (V): a place where stone axes could be procured. This was evidently a trade or barter centre. The barter lines extended right across the continent from east to west and from north to south, and the goods were passed on from one tribe to another. In this way objects and materials which were in short supply or unobtainable at one place could be exchanged for local products, even though the places were hundreds of miles apart, and the intervening tribes spoke different languages. Each tribe or clan would be likely to know the language of the tribe next to it on either side, and in this way exchanges could be made over such long distances.

Larrawallup (V): a place where lizards lie or sleep.

Legerup (W): a place where kangaroos dance.

Leumeah (N): here I rest.

Leura (N): lava.

Lietelinna (N): a house or a place on the side of a hill.

Lillipilli (N): the myrtle; a tree with small edible berries.

Lirambenda (S): a creek with permanent water flow. Now Finke River.

-long (N): a suffix. It usually means a plain in New South Wales.

Lowalde (S): summer.

Lowanna (N): a girl.

Lridalah (Q): a fight over women.

Lurr (Q): lilies growing on a lagoon.

M

Maccalla (Q): full moon.

Madabareenah (W): plenty of trees and shallow water.

Madiwaitu (S): white flint. Now Maitland.

Magakine (W): trees close to the water's edge.

Maggea (S): a camp.

Mahyl (Q): sugar-bag (nest of the honey bee).

Mailidup (W): got sharp eyes.

Maira (Q): a finger.

Mairmudding (W): I will spear you.

Malabine (W): salt or brackish water.

Malagara (Q): lightning.

Malaraway (N): a creek.

Malaria (N): the sap of the apple tree.

Malbeling (W): to wink.

Malla (S): a swamp plant.

Mallannyingah (W): a pool deeply gouged out by running water.

Malleea (N): green paddocks.

Maloo (N): thunder.

Manaro (N): from *maneroo*, breasts of a woman, so named from the cone-shaped pinnacles in the vicinity.

Manattarulla (N): sad-looking. Now Mount Misery or Mount Solitary.

Mancarbine (W): a place where gum is found. The gum was used for affixing axe heads and knives to their handles.

Mandurah (W): from *mandjar*, a trading place. See *Larow*.

Mandurama or **Mandurrama** (N): a water hole.

Mangiri (W): a gum tree forest.

Mangoplah (N): people; people singing.

Mangurup (W): swampy ground.

Manilla (N): from *Muneela*, winding river; round about. The river pursues a tortuous course at this place.

Manimoril (N): red cedar.

Manjimup (W): rushes near a water hole.

Manly (N): although not an Aboriginal word, the name is included because the Aborigines here were considered "manly", and from this the suburb received its name.

Mannagining (W): a place where people meet to exchange names.

Mannaw (W): honey.

Manoora (S): a spring.

Mantung (S): a white man's camp.

Mara (N): a black duck.

Maraju (Q): a plain kangaroo.

Maralinga (S): thunder.

Marama (S): a white duck.

Maramba (N): better.

Marami Creek (Q): small shell-fish.

Marawell (N): very large.

Marbilling (W): wind.

Marbolup (W): plenty of black-boy sticks with honey.

Mardarweiry (W): a hill covered in black stones.

Marebone (N): a place of strong winds.

Mareeba (Q): the meeting of the waters. At one time known as Abbot Creek and Granite Creek.

Marianbone or **Merryanbone** (N): from *moorianbone*, plenty of cockatoos. It has also been rendered as: see what a lot of cockatoos there are here.

Marinna (N): a song.

Markaling (W): friends.

Marlee (N): an elder tree.

Marleyquachyockup (W): swans alighted here.

Marlomerrikan or **Marloomerrikan** (N): thunder hole.

Marloognunah (W): plenty of shade.

Marnyong (N): a camp.

Marogi (N): a tree struck by lightning.

Marooan (N): something good.

Maroochy (Q): a black swan. See *Nindherry*.

Marook (N): good.

Maroubra Bay (N): from *merooberah*, the tribe which occupied this locality; or from *mouroubah*, a place where shells are found. Another meaning is thunder.

Marracoonda (W): leaning towards the west.

Marradong (W): a burnt log.

Marralmeedah (N): it was believed by the local Aborigines that this was the first place to be created on earth.

Marrangaroo (N): little blue flowers.

Marrapigup or **Marripigup** (W): where a man broke his hand.

Marrar (N): a tarantula spider.

Marree (S): a place of possums.

Marreyourga (N): a flat rock in the shape of a man's hand.

Marrilman (N): dwarf honeysuckle.

Marulan (N): from *murrawoollan*.

Marumba (Q): good.

Mashbalgadjerry (W): kangaroo stuck in the rock.

Mathinna (T): the name of an Aboriginal girl who was befriended by the Governor, Sir John Franklin.

Mathoura (N): from *mathowra*, windy.

Matong (N): from *matong*, strong or powerful. The story is that an Aboriginal here displayed unusual strength.

Mayurra (S): from *maayera*, fern stalks.

Meannjin (Q): the Aboriginal name for Brisbane from the bridge round to the creek. It has been recorded that a Turribul tribesman would say: *Meannjin utta yarranar*, I'm going to Brisbane.

Mebboonignarlinup (W): a man with crooked knees.

Mecrano (N): bushes.

Medulegah (N): the nest of the honey bee.

Meebalbogan (Q): a watcher on the mountain. Now Mount Greville.

Meee (N): stars.

Meekinhindunpup (W): moon climbing up the sky.

Megalong (N): the valley under the cliff. Now Medlow Bath.

Meinya (W): a centipede.

Meleymaning (W): a place where ghosts are seen.

Melinga (N): plenty.

Mel Mel (N): eyes. Now Great Island.

Melnar (Q): a fly.

Melnunni (N): red ground. Now Hillston.

Menangle (N): from *menangel*, large lagoon or swamp.

Menigup (W): an edible red root.

Menindie (N): the yolk of an egg.

Meningie (S): mud.

Meprupiping (V): a clump of trees where wasps build their nests.

Merah (N): from *mera*, left-handed people.

Mercadool (N): from *mookadool*, blind; or the place of small oaks.

Mercowie (S): clear water. Now Crystal Brook.

Meriamunka (N): bones.

Merilup (W): a place for making woomeras.

Merimbula (N): from *merimboola* or *murrumboola*, a place of large snakes; place of two waters or lakes.

Merinda (N): a beautiful woman.

Meriwolt (Q): a pigeon.

Mermerrah (Q): a young woman.

Mernmerna (S): buttocks.

Merrewa (N): pretence; sham.

Merrgining (W): where people meet to count their fingers.

Merri (N): a dingo. There are many places in New South Wales which incorporated this word. Five of them follow.

Merribegia (N): plenty of dingoes.

Merribooka (N): a dead dingo.

Merrigal (N): plenty of dingoes.

Merrigang (N): the place of dingoes.

Merri Merri (N): dingoes.

Merrina (N): plenty of grass seed and flour. Where the grass grew profusely the seed was gathered and ground to flour. Such a locality would be highly prized.

Merringurra (Q): plenty of kangaroos.

Merroing (N): a carpet snake.

Merryanbone (N): see *Marianbone*.

Merrygining (W): a place frequented by an evil spirit.

Merrygoen (N): a bleeding nose.

Merrywinebone (N): plenty of cockatoos.

Merungora (N): the stump of a box tree.

Mia Creek (N): a small creek.

Miamia (V): a hut; many huts; a camp.

Miandetta (N): the bend in a river.

Micabil (N): a tree struck by lightning.

Mickalamp (W): a large swamp.

Micke (N): a tree struck by lightning.

Mickelloo (Q): a white man.

Micketeeboomulgeiai (Q): a place where lightning has struck. Another form of the name *miketymulga* is found in New South Wales, where *miki* means lightning. *Miketymulga* means a tree struck by lightning.

Mickibri (N): the place of lightning.

Midgee (N): a small grassy plain.

Midgee (Q): small.

Miena (N): beside a lagoon.

Migeengum (Q): a cane which grows in this locality.

Mil (N): an eye. A word which enters into at least twenty place names in New South Wales.

Milai (Q): a shrub or tree.

Milamunda (N): a lazy person (an expression of contempt).

Milang (S): from *milangk*, a place where black magic is practised.

Milbong (Q): eye gone away. The Aborigines gave the name because of a one-eyed shepherd who lived here. The place was also known as One Eye's Waterhole.

Milbrulong (N): a rosella parrot.

Mildura (N): from *dura* or *cura*, a fly; *mil*, the eye: a place where sore eyes are prevalent, no doubt caused by flies that could not easily be driven off.

Milgin Milgin (N): a sparrow hawk.

Miliabacoolah (Q): the meeting of two sandhills.

Milina (W): paper bark trees.

Milingandi (N): a place of pipeclay.

Millagun (Q): a spear in the eye.

Millamurra (N): many eyes.

Millelung (V): a water hen.

Millgetta (Q): a sulky woman.

Milliburingyango (N): a large mountain.

Millnegang (N): plenty of yams.

Mil Mil (N): many eyes.

Milparinka (N): water may be found here; find a water hole here; where sore eyes are prevalent. See *Mildura*.

Milperra (M): company.

Mimosa (N): a place of wattle trees.

Minago (Q): what do you want?

Minane (N): the last man.

Minarcobrinni (N): take the feather out of the old pelican.

Minbalup (W): a happy place.

Mindaribba (N): a hunter.

Minemoorong (N): a camp.

Mingajibbi (W): plenty of ants.

Mingaletta (N): a bloodwood tree.

Minganup (W): plenty of rats.

Mingay (N): sick.

Minil (N): pretty girl; octopus.

Minimbah (N): from *minim*, teacher or elder; *bah*, place: the elders of the tribal council passed on their knowledge of tribal history and sacred lore to men as they passed through the various degrees of initiation.

Minlacowie (S): sweet water.

Minmi (N): a large lily.

Minnamurra (N): plenty of fish.

Minnegang: see *Mirregarng*.

Minnunggorana (N): why are you talking to me?

Minore (N): from *minawa*, where?; *minye*, why?; a white flower.

Minyagoyugilla (N): why are you crying? This was a large spring near the Namoi River.

Mirrabook (N): the constellation of the Southern Cross.

Mirragurra (N): a man coming across a wide plain.

Mirregarg (N): go back. Now Minnegang.

Mirribandini (N): dingoes fall down. A large kangaroo ripped open a dingo which was chasing it, and threw it down.

Mirrool (N): coloured clay or pigment.

Mitdapilly (Q): swampy gully.

Mittagong (N): from *mirragang*, a place where dingoes play. Other meanings are: little mountain; plenty of dingoes; a companion.

Mitta Mitta (V): thunder; little waters.

Mittegong (V): a magpie.

Mlonerabe (Q): to paint a hieleman or shield.

Mogil (N): a stone axe; wild pomegranate.

Mogil Mogil (N): a place where there was plenty of stone for making axes; the place of the wild pomegranates; the place where plenty of *bumble* or wild orange trees grow.

Mogo (N): pipeclay; a stone axe. Now Pipe Clay Creek.

Mogurah (N): to leave.

Moira (W): a ring-tail possum.

Mokeley (N): a wild orange tree.

Mokodabit (W): rain falling straight down.

Mollon (Q): cabbage trees.

Mollup (W): a large pool of water.

Molong (N): all rocks.

Momite (V): sun. There was a small mound of earth here, rather like an ant heap, on which the Aborigines placed sticks during the winter, setting fire to them in the spring. This form of sympathetic magic was designed to make the sun shine brightly during the summer months.

Monache (W): a white cockatoo with a red tail.

Monaro (N): from *maneroo*, a woman's breasts; or possibly from the same word, meaning a plain. This district was first called Brisbane Downs.

Monarto (S): the name of an Aboriginal woman who lived in the locality.

Moneal Moneal (N): an oyster.

Mongarumba (N): two camps close together.

Mongoluring (W): plenty of shade.

Moobalinbah (N): a log high above the ground.

Mooball (N): bowels; lake.

Moobeencultak (Q): an old man.

Moobor (Q): a rat.

Moochingoo (Q): a dead man.

Moodyarrup (W): a deep pool.

Moogal (N): a pretty girl.

Moogenallin (W): a peculiar smell.

Moogoon (N): a beetle.

Moojebing (W): plenty of *moojung* birds.

Moojoey (Q): a bone.

Mookerawa (N): ironbark trees.

Mooki (N): blind.

Mookimawybra (N): creek; fire; stone axe.

Mookimba (W): a white lake.

Moolabulla (W): plenty of beef.

Moolcha (Q): lancewood tree.

Mooldup (W): a shady place.

Moolpa (N): a black duck.

Moombahlene or **Moombahline** (N): from *moombah*, blowing, *lene*, to leave alone: probably meaning to make a noise. Now Tenterfield.

Moombarriga (N): a native cherry tree.

Moombindoo (N): a quail.

Moombooldool (N): from *moom*, death.

Moomoom (Q): ridges.

Moonan (N): something difficult to do.

Moonavinbinbie (N): a place where a man hit a kangaroo on the back with a stick and killed it.

Moonbil (N): a greenhead ant. Now Aberdeen.

Moondah (V): a black snake.

Moondarrewa (Q): from *moonjerabah*, a mosquito.

Moondoo (Q): mud.

Moonkoon (Q): a place where plenty of wallabies can be obtained.

Moonoo (N): a water rat.

Moonoomgah (N): tea-tree.

Moonta (S): from *moonterra*, a place of impenetrable scrub.

Moonyugin (N): a mountain of vermin.

Moopoo (Q): to cut.

Moora (N): nose.

Moorak (S): a mountain.

Moorine (W): bread.

Mooroduc (V): a dark and swampy place.

Moorombunnia (N): a hill where all the trees are burnt off.

Mooroobie (Q): death adders.

Moorungum (N): water weed.

Moppin (N): thigh.

Moramana (N): a bad place for firewood.

Morambro (S): from *marampo*, a place of wattle birds.

Morandoo (N): the sea.

Morangarel (N): a water fowls' nest.

Morborup (W): been a large rock.

Mordinup (W): a swamp.

Mordiyallock (V): running water.

Moree (N): a long spring; water hole; a stone.

Morgyup (W): a hill where stone was procured for making axes.

Morialta (S): ever-flowing.

Morongla (N): a crayfish.

Moronobin (W): a big corroboree.

Mororo (N): a fighting place.

Mortalup (W): a sandy beach.

Morundah (N): I got in the mud.

Moruya (N): a place down south; a water crossing.

Moto (N): from *mutuh*, a black snake.

Mourabimerri (N): a view from a hill. Now Mount Lookout.

Mourrindoc (N): a nulla nulla.

Moutaree (N): a flood in the creek.

Mowbardonemargodine (W): where the wombats fight.

Mowla (N): shade.

Mowonbymoney (N): big rapid water. Now the Snowy River.

Moyekaeeta (N): a dead dog. Now Dead Dog Beach.

Muckiwinnormbin (N): a ghost. Now Myrtle Creek.

Mudah (N): breasts.

Mudamuckla (S): a water supply.

Mudgee (N): contented; a nest. This place was noted for the number of birds' nests found there.

Mudgeerabah (Q): a place where lies were told.

Mudieyarra (S): fish holes.

Mudjimba (Q): see *Nindherry*.

Mugerne (Q): a perch (fish).

Mugga (N): a diamond snake. Now Long Bay.

Muggi (N): a porcupine.

Muggora (N): winter.

Mugimullen (N): can't go to sleep.

Mugra (N): a house hidden by vegetation.

Mukintundunrup (W): the moon rising above the hills.

Mularabone (N): muddy water.

Mulcurriberry (Q): full of devil-devils. the place was reputed to be the haunt of evil spirits.

Mulgarnup (W): a cold place.

Mulgawarrina (N): many mulga trees standing up.

Mulgowrie (N): one place for water.

Mulgranah (Q): where roots are dug for food.

Mulgulgum (N): the wild raspberry.

Mulgunnia (N): one hut.

Mulkblourway (N): milk and flour given away.

Mullawerring (W): plenty of mountain devils.

Mullion Creek (N): from *mullian* or *mullyan*, an eagle-hawk.

Mullock (V): the stinging nettle. Now Branxholm.

Mullumbimby (N): a small round hill.

Mulubinba (N): the place of the *mulubin* fern. Now Newcastle.

Mulumba (Q): rocks here.

Mulwala (N): rain.

Mulyan (N): a place where the eagle-hawks congregate.

Mulyanjandera (V): from *mulyan*, eagle-hawk; *jandera*, nesting place: the nesting place of the eagle-hawks.

Mumbil (N): a black wattle.

Mumblebone (N): from *mumble*, native beech; *bone*, place of; the name may be rendered: place of *mumble* trees, and has even appeared as: see what a lot of *mumble* trees are here. An alternative explanation has also been provided: from *mumbobone*, many beetwood trees.

Munagin (W): plenty of snakes near a lake.

Munayang (N): a place where corroborees are held.

Munbilla (Q): plenty of water.

Mundamutti (N): home of a solitary man. It has been said that an Aboriginal lived here alone and refused to go walkabout with his fellow tribesmen.

Mundanup (W): a high hill.

Mundi (N): a place where water may be found.

Mundi Mundi (N): a place where there is much permanent' water.

Mundoora (S): floods bring fish.

Mundowery (N): possibly from *mundowey*, a foot.

Mungahwakaah (N): from *mungah*, ants; *wakaah*, a creek.

Mungalkolli (N): from *mungal*, running; *kolli*, water: running water.

Mungarra (Q): a gum tree.

Mungarry (Q): an eagle-hawk.

Mungee (N): a native willow.

Mungerabah (Q): a sandy headland.

Mungeribah (N): red clay.

Mungery (N): from *moongery*, red or black sticky mud or clay.

Mungiebundie (N): lizards popping up.

Mungindie (N): a water hole in the river.

Mungon (Q): a girl.

Mungungboora or **Mungungcoorra** (N): a bulrush. Now Fine Flower Creek.

Mungyer (N): from *mungyor*, a tree growing on the bank of a creek or swamp; a big lagoon.

Munkel Munkel (N): a place where oysters were eaten.

Munmurra or **Munmarra** (N): a moon-mad or moon-blind Aboriginal.

Munna (N): flat; wide.

Munnungngurraba (N): a place of the sea snipe.

Murdong (W): ripe wild peaches.

Murengeriga (N): a wattle tree.

Murgah (N): a cuckoo.

Murgon (N): a mushroom.

Murnal (V): plenty of dust; sandy country.

Murninni (N): a large dried-up lake.

Muronbong (N): night.

Murrabinna (S): a stony, scrubby place.

Murrabrine, Murrabaine, or **Murrooburine** (N): from *murra*, hand; *ba*, place of; *ine*, a contraction of *mine*, meaning man: as the Aborigines put up both hands to indicate a large number, the name can be translated as a number of men gathered together.

Murrabungalgie (N): a hand hit on hand.

Murracompagoorandannie (N): a person whose hand has been cut off.

Murragang (N): a young man; a playground.

Murragoedgoen (N): bleeding hands.

Murragonga (N): very small men.

Murragurra (Q): drowned.

Murrami (N): a crayfish.

Murrarogan (N): frost.

Murrarundi (N): five finger.

Murrawan (N): one hand.

Murrawombie (N): a spear projecting from a tree. The significance of the expression is that it differentiates something thrown by the hand, *murra*, from a branch of the tree.

Murray (N): hurry.

Murrobo (N): thunder.

Murrooburine (N): see *Murrabrine*.

Murrowolga (N): a long reach of deep water.

Murrumba (Q): good.

Murrembidgee or **Murrumbidgee** (N): big water; plenty of water; a track goes down here. It has been suggested that all rivers in this locality were called by this name because the word meant ever-flowing.

Murrumbong (N): a good place for game.

Murrumburrah (N): two canoes on the way to the *bora* ground.

Murrumurro (Q): the sound made by the plain turkey.

Murrungundie (N): from *moora milldegindeginduy*, nose and eyes at play. The expression therefore really means: laughing.

Murrurundi (N): five fingers; a mountain.

Murtoa (V): home of the lizard.

Murumba (Q): good.

Murwillumbah (N): several explanations are offered: from *murri*, people; *wolli*, camp; *bah*, place of; from *murra*, big or many; *willum*, possums; *bah*, place of. To the meanings of place where many people are encamped, and the place where there are many possums, we may add: camp site; and the name of the local tribe. See *Quinyum Quinyum*.

Musero (W): no-good place where bad people go.

Mushwandry (W): good place where good people go.

Muteroo (W): no-good place.

Mutooroo (S): place to go to for food.

Muttama (N): take it.

Myalla (N): from *pyalla*, big talk; to talk.

Myambat (N): a hut.

Myallmundi (N): one tree.

Myamyu (V): see *Tharnkur-ruckkulk*.

Myangup (W): an echo.

Myeah (Q): father.

Mymuggine (W): a flat rock in a gully. A rock of this kind would be treasured because it would hold water.

Myoon Myooan (N): red and yellow stones which provide pigment for body decoration.

Myponga (S): from *malppinga*, a divorced wife.

N

Na (N): to see.

Nabelmup (W): a gully with a running stream.

Nabiac (N): a wild fig tree.

Nackara (S): a combination of words meaning brother, and looking eastwards.

Nadda (S): a camp.

Nadjongbilla (N): from *nadjong*, water; *billa*, creek. Permanent or running water.

Nahvoung (Q): mother.

Naliandrah (V): a butterfly.

Nallabooma (N): pine trees growing on the sandhills.

Nalloor (Q): crayfish.

Namalata River (Q): a messenger. Named by Nicholas Hey, a Bavarian missionary to the Aborigines.

Nambour (Q): tea-tree; flame tree; tea-tree bark; red-flowering tea-tree.

Nambucca River and Heads (N): crooked river; entrance to the sea. Derived from *ngambugka*, literally entrance to the waters.

Nammoona (N): milk.

Namogit (N): a quarry. Certain rock quarries were prized for stone which was suited for making grinding stones, used in grinding seed to flour. Such stones became objects of trade over a wide area. Now Barrietown.

Namoi River (N): from *ngnamai* or *nygamai*, a species of acacia; or from *nynamu*, the breast, because the river here curves like a woman's breast.

Nampup (W): plenty of kangaroo teeth for making spear heads.

Nana Glen (N): from *nana*, a small lizard.

Nanardine (N): a swallow.

Nanegup (W): a swamp.

Nangar (N): bold mountain; red rocks. One peak on this mountain is precipitous and stands out boldly.

Nangarie (Q): a large fishing net.

Nangawooka (S): a place of springs. Now Hindmarsh valley.

Nangkita (S): a place of little frogs.

Nangwarry (S): from *nrang-ware*, a path to the cave.

Nanima or **Nanimi** (N): lost it; lost there; something lost there.

Nantabibbie (S): a black kangaroo.

Nantawarra (S): from *nurn-towerrah*, black kangaroo country.

Naodaup (W): what is the matter?

Nappamerril (N): a sandhill and water hole.

Naracoorte (S): from *gnange-kuri*, a large water hole.

Naraman (N): a long way behind.

Naranagi (N): a small creek.

Narang (N): a small creek.

Narara (N): a black snake.

Naratoola (N): a burial place.

Nardeeneen (N): he is in love.

Nardie (W): a hill beside a long pool of water.

Nardoowage (N): one stops, the other goes.

Nardu (N): from *nardoo*, the berry or seed from which women made flour.

Nargan (V): a cave inhabited by a spirit.

Nargong (N): light.

Nargoon or **Warnagoon** (V): native bear.

Nariah (N): a bare place on a hill.

Narkabunda (V): the sea at the back of the world.

Narooma (N): a zania palm growing in water; a magic stone. Stones, bones and quartz crystals were part of the properties of medicine men and sorcerers.

Narra- (N): a root word in at least thirty places in New South Wales, meaning forks, forked, twisted, turned about, black, or dark. Names which include this root and are still used: *Narrabarba*, *Narrabeen*, *Narrabri*, *Narraburra*, *Narrawa*, *Narrawin*, etc.

Narrabri (N): forks; forked sticks; big creek.

Narraburra (N): from *narra*, twisted; *burra*, stones: rough country.

Narrandera (N): a place of the goanna or blue-tongued lizard.

Narrawa (N): probably formed from the root word *narra*, q.v. Another opinion is that it is from *ngarrawah*, far away from the tribal centre.

Narriah (N): a bare place.

Narrie (N): a bush fire.

Narringbunkarrinup (W): a sand patch.

Narrogal (N): a place where honey is found.

Narromine (N): from *gnarrowmine*, a place for honey; a man carrying honey; or from *gnaroo*, bony; *mine*, a man: a bony man.

Narrung (S): from *ngnararung*, a place of the large she-oaks.

Narryer, Mount (W): the name of the Aboriginal who accompanied the surveyor R. Austin in 1854.

Nattai (N): water.

Naturi (S): sandy soil.

Navimbarra (Q): God (literally high master).

Nea (N): breasts.

Neago (N): possibly from *ngoorooko*, tomorrow.

Neenan (N): a grasshopper.

Neergoolabulgra (N): he kept it.

Neibichup (W): freshwater fish named coblers.

Nelaungaloo (N): a lizard.

Nelshaby (S): from *nelcebee*, boiling or bubbling springs.

Nendanup (W): the shape of a tail.

Nerang (Q): little.

Nerbichup (W): a bubbling stream.

Nermone (N): green paddocks.

Nerrigundah (N): a camp where edible berries are found.

Newee Creek (N): from the *Newee Newee* tribe.

Newmoonta (S): *moonta* is an abbreviated form of *moonterra*, a place of impenetrable scrub.

Ngarroinba (N): a place of female emus.

Ngeatalling (W): a possum in a hollow tree.

Nhill (V): possibly from *nyell*, a place of spirits.

Niangala (N): an eclipse of the moon.

Nigigin (W): a small spring.

Nijong (N): a drink; water.

Nikkinba (N): from *nikkin*, coal: a place of coal.

Nimbin or **Nimboon** (N): pointed rock; small rocky peak.

Nimbuwah (Q): standing alone.

Nimmitabel (N): from *nimoitebool*, a place where many waters meet; the source of many streams. Over the years there have been a number of interesting changes in the spelling and pronunciation of the name: Nimitybell; Nimithy Bale; Nimmitabelle.

Nimoola (N): a steep slope.

Ninacoogerup (W): a place where a number of creeks run together.

Nindherry, Mount (Q): according to the local legend Nindherry, an old man, was jealous of Coolum, a much younger man, because he had made advances to his wife Maroochy. He threw a stone at him and knocked off his head, which became Mudjimba Island. Maroochy was apparently the name of Nindherry's wife, and the name Coolum ought therefore have been given to the island, as it was the young man's head that was transformed into an island.

Nindooimba (Q): a snake creeping along the ground.

Ningana (S): to rest.

Nioka (N): a green hill.

Nirrittiba (N): a place of mutton birds.

Noarlunga (S): a fishing place.

Nocuting (W): a place where men meet for sacred ceremonies. No women were allowed near the *bora* ground.

Nomenade Creek (Q): a pine tree. At one time it was known as Pine Creek.

Nooan (Q): brother.

Noogoon (Q): a yam. Now St Helena Island.

Noona (N): from *ngoonan*, a place where a mopoke was killed.

Noora (S): a camp.

Noorengong (V): a magpie.

Nooroo (N): dark.

Noorooma (N): a sacred stone belonging to the Kooragee tribe.

Norogo (N): a black kangaroo.

Norring (W): a long way off; distant.

Noueboondie (N): a round hill.

Nounmoning (W): wet country.

Nourani (N): no rain here.

Nownorrup (W): a headland.

Nowra (N): a black cockatoo; two; you and me.

Noyumboon (N): a platypus. Later called *Woodenbong*.

Nubba (N): a child.

Nubhoygum (N): to hold; to cling. The name was given because the lawyer vine grew so thickly here.

Nubingerie (N): a young man.

Nudgee (Q): a green frog.

Nugoon (Q): nephew. Now St Helena Island.

Nulcrawontharena (W): onion brother, a small onion-like plant.

Nulla Nulla (N and Q): a war club.

Nulungery (N): a clever-man or medicine-man, a native "doctor".

Numby (N): from *ngumby*, a sleeping place.

Numby Numby (N): from *ngumby ngumby*, very sleepy place.

Numeralla (N): a valley of plenty.

Numira (N): a place of reeds,

used in the making of dilly bags.

Numminbah (Q): a place of small palms.

Numulgi (N): a scrub turkey.

Numurkah (V): a shield used in fighting.

Nunagin (W): plenty of snakes near a lake.

Nunda (Q): a mulberry tree.

Nundah (N): wood; a river with good water.

Nundah (Q): mouth; a chain of water holes; north.

Nundahurrah (N): a river crossing a plain.

Nundryculling (W): branches of trees.

Nungattah (N): a place of mourning.

Nungeroo (W): whiskers.

Nunjikompita (S): a water hole.

Nunkeri (S): beautiful.

Nunnook (N): a corner.

Nunyahboogera (W): my country.

Nurragi (S): scrub.

Nurrungbah (N): a place of the long-nosed shark.

Nutheramnatherann (N): a pleasant valley. Now Rose Valley.

Nyaparrlenye (Q): a stingray.

Nyjong (N): water.

Nyngan (N): a crayfish; a mussel; a place of many streams; a purple beetle.

Nyrang (N): small.

O

-o (V): a suffix meaning mountain or highland in Victoria.

Oah (Q): to talk.

Obley (N): where reeds bend over the water.

Ogeea (Q): fish.

Oimah (Q): a white man.

Ollpin (N): plenty of oaks for shelter near a big plain.

Omeo (N): mountains.

Onaunga (S): a large water hole.

-ong (N): a suffix meaning a permanent spring of water in New South Wales.

Ongunajha (Q): a white man speared.

Onkaparinga River (S): several explanations have been offered to account for this intriguing name: *ponke-porringa*, shadows in the water; *unkaparinga*, *ingang-kiparri*, and *ungkeperringa*, meaning another river, plentiful. The *Australian Encyclopaedia*, while recording *onkaga* as mother river, plentiful, states that it seems probable that the correct name was *ngankiparri*, woman's river, from the fact that when the Murray River tribes came to raid the local ochre mines the Noarlunga Aborigines hid their women in a place called *Nganki-parri-unga*, place of the

women's river, on the Onkaparinga before going out to
fight.

Onnua (Q): white man with gun.

Onua (Q): a Chinaman.

Oodlawirra (S): a weapon.

Oodnadatta (S): from *utnadata*,
the yellow flower of the
mulga tree. The place was
named by Sir Thomas Way.

Oodthulby (N): a place where
the reeds bend over the
water.

Oolambulla (Q): plenty of
grasshoppers.

Ooldea (S): meeting place
where water is available.

Oolong (N): a swampy plain.

Oomcurry (N): darkness; night.

Oondooroo (Q): low, prickly
scrub.

Ooringuldain (N): from *oorin*,
emu; *guldain*, lying there:
emu lying there: Now
Wilson's Downfall.

Oowan (N): a *lillypilly* tree.

Orana (N): welcome.

Orara (N): the home of the
perch.

Orroroo (S): from *oorooroo*,
the name of the creek was
applied to the settlement.
When Sir Charles Todd was
Postmaster-General he said
that there was little point in
providing better postal
facilities as the place never
had more than two letters.

Oulnina (S): good water.

Oumbigalneeong (N): I met
him there.

Ourimbah (N): a *bora* or
ceremonial ground.

Ouyen (V): ghost water hole.

Owenyonni (N): *colberry* emu.

P

Pachomai (N): grey.

Padulla (N): a stone.

Pallal (N): a creek.

Pallano (Q): the new moon.

Pamandi (N): the wife of an
uncle. There is a distinction
between uncle's wife and
aunt. The wife by marriage
would belong to another
moiety.

Pambula (N): two waters.

Para River (S): from *pari*, a
stream of water.

Parachilna (S): a river with a
stony bed and steep banks.

Parairie, Mount (NT): far away,
distant. Named by Michael
Terry the explorer.

Parakylia (S): a succulent plant.

Parattah (T): ice.

Parilla (S): cold.

Paringa (S): a whirlpool.

Parragundi (N): distant parrots.

Parrakie (S): underground
water.

Parramatta (N): several explanations have been given:
head of the river; the place
where the eels lie down; a
dark jungle.

Parraweena (N): parrots' camping place.

Paruna (S): a stopping place. Named by Governor Galway in 1914.

Pata (S): swamp gum trees.

Patawalonga (S): a swampy stretch of water with many fish.

Patawilya (S): a green swampy place. Now Glenelg.

Patchieroombadillie (N): a good plain amongst the sandhills.

Patchiewarra (N): good berries.

Pathur (W): a mine or well.

Patonga (N): a small wallaby.

Peddybang (V): an emu.

Peedver (Q): ears.

Pendicup (W): plenty of red bottle-brush flowers.

Penola (S): from *penaoorla*, a swamp.

Penterong (N): a root with medicinal properties.

Perinyelup (W): a lobster found here.

Perponda (S): plains.

Piatarrja (Q): a waterhole where fish are found.

Pichirichi Pass (S): from *pitchery* or *pitjuri*, the leaves of a tree which were chewed and had a narcotic effect. Formerly Richman's Pass.

Pikapene (N): the bark used for making coolamons.

Pilliga (N): from *billarga*, a place of swamp oaks.

Pilliga (N): from *biligha*, head of scrub oak.

Pimbaacla (S): plenty of pine trees.

Pimpama (Q): the place of the peeweet.

Pindari (N): high ground.

Pinduro (W): waves of the sea.

Pini (N): a vine lying on the ground.

Pinkee (Q): a bottle tree.

Pinkenbah (Q): a place of freshwater turtles.

Pinnaroo (S): a widely used term in South Australia for an old man, elder, or one with considerable status.

Pinneena (N): a good place to catch water and to keep it for future needs.

Pirralea (N): fishing.

Pirrama (N): a rocking stone. Now Pyrmont.

Pirrin (N): a cave.

Pitchicanana (Q): plenty of mussels.

Piththunga or **Piththungnar** (N): a place with plenty of oysters.

Pitoba (N): a place of pipeclay.

Pitonga (N): from *pita*, snake; *tonga*, mangrove tree. There was an accident here involving both a snake and a mangrove tree.

Pokataroo (N): a river going wide.

Polona (N): a hawk.

Pomand, Point (S): from *pommundi*.

Poonboon (V): a bittern; heron.

Pooncaira (N): a large sand-hill.

Pooraka (N): a turpentine tree.

Poormungburrh (V): named after the headman of the local tribe. Now Digby.

Pothana (N): smoke.

Prahran (V): partly surrounded by water.

Pucawan (N): a native bear.

Pulbging or **Pullgin** (N): a bone in the kangaroo's leg. Now Gordon Brook.

Pulchra (Q): a water hole frequented by pelicans.

Pullabooka (N): from *pulla*, head.

Pulletop (N): taking up a tree.

Pullgin (N): see *Pulbing*.

Punchumgum (Q): a native cat.

Pungonda (S): a fight.

Punkally (N): you are greedy.

Puntapin (W): many rocky hills.

Puntei (N): a narrow place or point of lane.

Puntpuntpundaloo (N): a bell-bird.

Puranga (Q): grey hair; flour bag.

Purkaburra (Q): the name of the local tribe.

Purpur (N): a *bora* ground where initiation rites are performed.

Purpur (V): a creek where there are plenty of turtles.

Purribangla (N): a place of ants'

nests. A powdery yellow substance was obtained from the nests and used as pigment for body painting.

Purryburry (N): a boys' playground.

Pwooyam (N): a sleeping lizard. Now Lismore South.

Pyree (N): a place of box trees.

Q

Quaama (N): shallow water.

Quabathoo (N): from *coabathoo*, a topknot pigeon.

Quaberup (W): a good lake.

Quabin (W): a good camp.

Quabothoo or **Guabothoo** (N): the call of the pigeon. There were many pigeons in this district.

Quagerup (Q): an edible root.

Quamara (Q): hunting.

Quamby (Q): to stop; a camp.

Quamby (V): from *quambyoot*, to settle down, rest, or sleep.

Quandialla (N): a porcupine.

Quandline (W): plenty of large trees.

Quangulmerang (V): a place where honey is found.

Quarbing (W): a good place.

Quaringa (Q): an island.

Quatquatta (N): plenty of fish.

Quean (N): very tall trees growing here.

Queanbeyan (N): clear water.

Queerbri (N): fish swim quick. This is a sharp bend in the Namoi River where the water flows swiftly.

Queeryourga (N): a freshwater creek containing mussels.

Quelquang (W): a large sandy plain.

Quidong (N): from *cooedong*, the place of the echo.

Quilbone (N): plenty of quail.

Quindalup (W): a happy place.

Quinginup (W): plenty of rats.

Quingmory (Q): a spoonbill duck.

Quingun (Q): a devil.

Quinyum Quinyum (N): a plant which resembles the wild belladonna. Now *Murwill-umbah*.

Quipolly (N): a creek where plenty of fish are found in the water holes.

Quirindi (N): from *guyer-warindi* or *guyerwarinda*, waters fall together; dead tree on a mountain top. The Surveyor-General Mitchell called it *Cuerindie*.

Quirinerup (W): plenty of bush kangaroos.

Quoak (V): a laughing jackass.

R

Ra (Q): the sun.

Rajah (Q): the stars.

Ramco (S): a contraction of *dogorampko*.

Rangal (Q): tea-tree.

Reka (N): this is not an Aboriginal word, but a Maori word imported from New Zealand, meaning sweet.

Renmark (S): red mud.

Rewring (Q): swans.

Roba (Q): plenty of goannas.

Robindalgar (Q): a black cockatoo.

Romerah (Q): an old man; elder.

Roolcarirultaduannaaram (N): one tree on a hill.

Royalberra (Q): plenty of hawks.

Rulwalla (N): a very large stone.

Rumbriah (N): a big mountain where the clans gather together.

Rungie (N): swans.

S

Sauming (Q): a place where a battle was fought.

Shara (Q): salt water.

Sheringa (S): yams. These plants grew abundantly here.

Sparindeen (Q): plenty of turtles.

Starra or **Stura** (Q): an iron-stone ridge.

T

Tabbigong (N): a fish.

Tabboo (N): a small boy.

Tabby Tabby Island (Q): a small crab.

Tabrabucca (N): place where

the bora rites were performed.

Tabragalba (Q): the forgotten nulla nulla.

Tabulam (N): my native home; my native country.

Taengarrahwarrawarildi (N): the place of the yellow-jacket trees.

Tagboin (N): a bandicoot.

Tahmoor (N): a bronze-wing pigeon.

Taja (Q): head.

Takumuna (N): a house on a rise.

Talarook (V): a wattle bird; honeysucker.

Taldra (S): a kangaroo.

Taleeban (N): new.

Talia (S): near water.

Tallagandra (N): a place where crows are plentiful.

Tallah (Q): a pandanus tree.

Tallangatta (V): many trees.

Tallawang (N): the native apple.

Tallawarra (N): slippery place.

Tallebudgera (Q): a man bitten by a shark.

Tallimba (N): a young man.

Tallong (N): a tongue; a tongue of land (peninsula); a spring of water.

Talofa (N): this is not an Aboriginal word, but comes from the Samoan: rejoicing and goodwill.

Taloumbi (N): a windy place.

Talwalpin (Q): a place of cotton trees.

Talwurrapin (Q): a hibiscus tree.

Formerly Redland Bay.

Tamalee (W): lie down on your belly.

Tamban (N): a place of wiry grass.

Tambaroora (N): a place of the ibis.

Tambo (Q): fish; yam.

Tamborine (Q): from *tchambreen*, a wild lime tree.

Tamplagooda (W): to fall down, an expression used of a precipitous cliff.

Tanbil (N): collar-bone.

Tangorron (N): no water; dry.

Tantanoola (S): possibly from *tantanoorla*, a brushwood shelter, either a simple hut or a breakwind. Another theory is that it comes from Malay and means boggy.

Tanunda (S): plenty of wild-fowl.

Taplan (S): grass trees.

Tappin Tappin (N): shoal water.

Taragoro (S): a small black shag. The name was given by Governor Galway in 1914.

Taralga (N): a native companion.

Tarampa (Q): a place of wild limes.

Tarana (N): a large water hole.

Tarboonenltak (Q): a white man.

Tarboonkinkill (Q): a white woman.

Tarboonpooliman (Q): a white policeman.

Tarcoola (N): a river bend.

Tarcoola (S): this was not the original Aboriginal name. The place was named after the winner of the Melbourne Cup in 1893.

Tarcowie (S): washaway water.

Tarcutta (N): flour and the cakes made from grass seed.

Tarebarre (Q): beautiful, sometimes used in the sense of "a pretty picture".

Taree (N): from *tarrebit* or *tarreebin*, a wild fig tree.

Targan (N): white.

Taronga Park (N): *taronga*, a beautiful view.

Taroom (Q): a wild lime tree.

Tarparrie (S): a muddy creek. Now Port Pirie.

Tarpeena (S): from *tartpena*, a red gum tree.

Tarraganda or **Tarragunda** (N): chain of pools; wild turkey.

Tarrana (N): a place where a woman was ravaged.

Tarrawatta (S): plenty of water.

Tarrawonga (N): a meeting place for pigeons.

Tarrego Moonbung Goonine (N): what country do you come from?

Tarro (N): a stone.

Tarup (W): a river named after the spear heads of the hunters.

Tarwonga (W): water running into a hole.

Tatham (N): baby; child; a woman with child; the latter meaning referred to a large gum tree growing here. It had a small trunk near the base, swelled into a large barrel in the middle, and had scanty top foliage, thus being said to resemble a pregnant woman.

Tathra (N): from *tatiara*, beautiful country; a place of native cats.

Tatiara (S): good country.

Tatuali (N): a swelling or excrescence on a tree which was cut off and scooped out to form a coolamon.

Teckerrygorry (Q): willy wagtail.

Teemenaar (Q): a spider.

Teerawah (Q): an angry rainbow. This probably had some connection with belief in the Rainbow Snake, the spirit which brought water in abundance when it was placated but caused droughts if it was offended.

Te Kowai (Q): not an Aboriginal but a Maori word meaning the *kowhai*, a tree with beautiful yellow flowers.

Tellegaree (N): a pelican.

Temagog (N): a wasp.

Temagong (N): land of the grasshopper.

Tempe (N): not an Aboriginal word but named after an

early residence called Tempe House. *Tempe* was derived from a Greek word meaning narrow valley.

Teralba (N): a place where edible plants grow.

Terrabulla (Q): beautiful ground.

Terragong (N): from *therrongungh*, a place where vines are collected.

Terramungamine (N): from *therramungermine* or *dhirrangbunganmine*, *dhirrang*, thigh; *bungan*, broken, *mine*, man: a man with a broken thigh; very stony ground.

Terranora (N): a small river; estuary.

Terrie Terrie (V): sandmartin.

Terrigal (N): a place of little birds.

Teta (Q): plenty of small black ants.

Thaahmarlkeepenk or **Thaahmarlkupenk** (V): the name of an invisible spirit with sharp projecting elbows who drives people mad by prodding them with his elbows. Now Drumberg.

Thabbat or **Tubbut** (V): the liver of an animal.

Thabbo (N): a boy; small.

Thahtoochthashurl or **Thahtoochthaahurrl** (V): cutting grass. Now Coleraine.

Thallmoy (N): big man eat plenty.

Tharah (Q): thunder; wind.

Thargobang (N): an old woman.

Thargomindah (Q): a porcupine.

Tharnkurruckkulk (V): from *tharn*, a road; *kurruckkulk*, an edible plant. Now Myamyu.

Thelim (S): a bend in the river. Now corrupted to Tailem Bend.

Thingabargan (V): a stone axe.

Thinggurrhmin (V): the name of the headman of the local tribe. Now Merino.

Thinnungwille (N): a foot like a possum's.

Thirroul (N): a hollow; a valley.

Thoar (Q): sunrise.

Thomar (Q): a small river.

Thoowata (Q): a big flood.

Thuddungra (N): water rushing down.

Thulengar (N): saltbush plains.

Thulley (Q): crows walking.

Thullugnethgie (N): a place for making spears.

Thullutheroey (N): with many spears.

Thuntalbi (N): from *tuntalbin*, a scrub pheasant; dilly bag.

Thureel (N): summer.

Thurgoona (N): from *thurgoon*, earth.

Thurlgona (Q): rocky; rocky soil.

Thurlgoona (N): dingo evacuating.

Thurre (N): a wild fig tree.

Thurrungo (Q): be quick; hurry.

Tibarri (Q): an eye.

Tibooburra (N): a heap of granite rocks.

Tibrogargan (Q): a biting squirrel.

Tickera (S): marshmallows.

Tidnacornarrinna (N): your foot and hand.

Tierabeenba (N): from *tira*, tooth: a tooth-like point of land.

Tilba Tilba (N): many waters.

Tillabudgery (N): a good view or outlook.

Tillararra (Q): a nest of springs.

Tillery (Q): a creek with thick scrub.

Timbarra or **Timbarrah** (N): a grass tree; a tree-fern.

Timbrebongey (N): from *timbrebonganj*, the broken breast of an emu.

Tinaroo (Q): not an Aboriginal name. An explanation that has been offered, which may be accepted or rejected at the reader's pleasure, is that when tin was discovered in this locality, the discoverer shouted, "Tin! Harroo!"

Tinbin (Q): the north wind.

Tindarra (Q): shallow water.

Tingalpa (Q): from *tinalbah*, which in turn was derived from *tingalfat*, and *bah*, the place of.

Tingha (N): flat; level; beef.

Tingira (Q): the sea.

Tinnenburra (N): a porcupine; a water hole.

Tinonee (N): from *tinobah*, a shark.

Tintenbar (N): the right-hand creek.

Tintinara (S): from *tinyinlara*, the stars in the Belt of Orion, these stars being supposed to be a number of young men hunting kangaroos and emus in the sky.

Tippoorare (Q): from *tippooroo*, to breathe.

Tirranna or **Tiranna** (N): running water.

Titwinda (N): a hole in a rock.

Tobagangang (V): the place where there was an eagles' nest.

Tobbery (W): something dirty, e.g. muddy water.

Tocumwal (N): a deep hole. The local legend claimed that there was a hole in the river by the township which was bottomless, and also an underground stream which ran to "The Rock" seven miles away.

Togar (N): smoke.

Tollerin (W): bark stripped from a tree.

Tomago (N): sweet water.

Tomanbill (N): from *tomabil*, crooked timber.

Tomingley (N): from *tahmiengooli*, a piece of bark which looks like a death adder. This has been rendered "Look out, there's a death adder!"

Tomki (N): greedy.

Tondaburine (N): flints ("fire-stones") which were plentiful in this district.

Tonderbruine (N): ashes flying through the air.

Tongarobin (V): a beetle found floating on whirlpools in summer.

Tongarra (N): the place of the cabbage trees. The hearts of the cabbage tree heads were eaten by the Aborigines, so it has been suggested that Bread Flat could well be a literal translation.

Tongril (N): a possum.

Toobeah (Q): to point. A signpost here gave rise to the name.

Toodyay (W): from *Toodyeep*, the wife of Coondebung, an Aboriginal who accompanied G. F. Moore in his expedition in 1836.

Toogoolawa (Q): from *Tugulawa*, the name of a tribe; the place of the heart, because of its shape.

Tookayerta (S): swampy land.

Toolaburroo (N): the last of the water.

Toolamanang (N): short spear.

Toolijooa (N): a place of emus.

Toollabidjael (N): a split spear.

Tooloom (N): louse; head-louse; tick. There are two places of this name, one in the Drake district, the other in the Ulmarra district.

Toongabbie (N): near the water.

Toongi (N): a scrub turkey.

Toora (N): plenty of bandicoots.

Toora (S): a mallee hen.

Toorak (N): a swamp where tea-trees grow.

Tooraweenah (N): plenty of brown snakes.

Toorong (N): a leech.

Tootool (N): an extinct bird.

Toowacka (Q): a camp; a camp in which to sleep.

Toowong (Q): the note of the cockatoo.

Toowoomba (Q): there are several explanations of this name: from *tchwampa*, the swamp; from *toowoon*, or *choowoom*, the native melon which grew by the swamp; or from *toowoomba* itself, meaning water sit down, or underground water. Following the Aboriginal name, the settlement was first known as The Swamp, but it did not meet with universal favour. Archdeacon Glennie was one who disliked the name, and in 1852 he recorded the residence of the children he baptised as Toowoomba; the name was adopted officially in 1858.

Topiely (N): box trees with mistletoe growing on them.

Torcomoora (Q): a large mussel.

Towang (N): go away.

Towealgra (N): a dove.

Towradgi (N): from *kowradgi*, keeper of the sacred stones. These were probably increase stones which were an important part of the ritual which linked the people with the Dreamtime, and ensured that the food supplies would be plentiful.

Towrang (N): a shield.

Towri (N): the boundary of the tribal lands. Such boundaries were strictly defined. To go outside them was to leave the protection of the ancestral spirits and to be homeless. The rights of tribal territories were strictly guarded, and though in times of famine some latitude might be allowed to another tribe, no one would dare to raid a neighbouring territory for game without permission, or even to take a stick without the consent of the tribal owners.

Trangie (N): quick; quick intercourse.

Traralgon (V): a heron; a native companion.

Tregeagle (N): from *dirrigeagle*, a grass-like plant.

Trungley (N): a rock on which stone axes were sharpened.

Tuan (Q): a spear.

Tubbo (N): possibly from *tubba*, burnt earth used in body painting; gypsum. Gypsum was used by medicine men in rainmaking ceremonies.

Tubbul (N): a bone.

Tubbut (V): see *Thabbat*.

Tucki Tucki (N): a reed with edible roots.

Tuckurimbah (N): a junction of two creeks; a glutton. Now Lismore.

Tuggerah or **Tuggarah** (N): cold. There were three places of this name in New South Wales, each meaning cold or very cold.

Tuggernong (N): a long cold plain.

Tugrabakh (N): a place of ironbark trees.

Tugulawa (Q): the place of the heart. Now *Bulimba*.

Tugullinbah (N): a fishing ground.

Tugwantallaban (N): cracks in the soil.

Tulla (Q): a stick; a tree.

Tullalar (Q): a shallow crossing.

Tullibigeal (N): yarran wood spears; a place for splitting yarran wood spears.

Tumbarumba (N): from *rumba*, sound: sounding ground, hollow-sounding. The earth gave out a hollow sound when stamped on.

Tumbilmullah (N): a snake.

Tumbiumbi (N): a place of big trees.

Tumbulgum (N): a large fig tree.

Tumpoaba (N): a place of clay.

Tumut (N): from *doomat* or *doomut*, a camping place by the river.

Tunabidgie (N): a long spear.

Tundigup (W): a small spring of water.

Tungbung (N): a creek where there are platypuses.

Tunnimgah (N): a low bushy tree; a shrub.

Tuorodon (N): a mopoke in a log.

Turaku (Q): a comet.

Turella (N): water weeds.

Turilwa (N): a water lily.

Turrabirren (N): broken stone. Now Myall Creek.

Turrabom (N): a splinter.

Turrabumbene or **Turrabambene** (N): long grass. Now Purfleet.

Turramboyne (N): a temporary hunting camp.

Turramurra (N): high land; a creek.

Turranbar (N): from *turran*, a large jumper ant.

Turrawan (N): a grey magpie.

Turrongoouddi (N): bitten by a snake.

Turrumbi (N): see *Durrumbi*.

Turrumga (N): a place where dingoes are caught.

Turramtalone (Q): place where a large eel escaped over a waterfall.

Twanginna (Q): a young man.

Twonkwillingup (W): to listen; to look.

Tyabb (V): from *tyaba*, a worm.

Tyagarah or **Tyagurah** (N): open grass country.

Tyagong (N): a wombat.

Tycannah (N): to bring something.

Tye (Q): blind.

Tyeebin (N): a stinging tree. Now Teven.

U

Uambi (N): pine scrub.

Uardry (N): a yellow box tree.

Uga (Q): lame.

Ugerebar (N): a place where the shellfish named *ugeree* can be obtained.

Uki (N): an edible swamp fern root. The name was given to a mountain and also to a small lagoon in the Byron Bay district.

Ulah (N): a ripple on the water.

Ulamambri (N): a place where possums breed.

Ulandi (N): a big tree; a burning log.

Ulladulla (N): from *woolladoorh* or *ngulladulla*, a safe harbour. The place was once popularly called Holy Dollar.

Ullamulla (N): white gum trees.

Ulmarra (N): a turn or bend in the river.

Ulooloo (S): from *ulaloo*, a creek named by Captain Frome, and said to mean: water by two hills.

Uloom (N): dry land. The locality received its name because it always remained above the level of the water when the rest of the district was flooded.

Umbango (N): to gaze at.

Umberumberka (N): a rat hole.

Umboodee (N): big mountain eels in the nearby river.

Umpiebong (Q): a deserted camp. First named Redcliffe Point, but when the settlement and the buildings were deserted the Aborigines promptly called it *umpie bong*.

Umungah or **Unumgar** (N): a place infested with lizards.

Unanderra (N): a junction of two creeks.

Ungar (Q): a beard.

Ungarie (N): a thigh.

Unnaro (W): a place of bob-tailed goannas.

Unumgar (N): see *Umungah*.

-up (W): a common place name termination in Western Australia.

Uraidla (S): from *yureidla*, a place of ears.

Uralba (N): a place with plenty of quartz stones; a home

between the hills; a hollow.

Uralla (N): a big hill; by-and-by.

Urana (N): from *wahrinah* or *wirrinah*, the noise made by quails as they rise from the ground. Quails were plentiful in this district.

Urangbil (N): leaves.

Uranquinty, Uranna, or **Uran-geline** (N): the yellow box tree, so named because of its colour when the bark is stripped off. These trees provided a home for fat, sweet grubs which were a favourite article of diet. Also plenty of rain.

Urawilkie (N): long grass.

Uringa or **Urunga** (N): a long beach.

Urrabirra (S): to swallow.

Urrugalgee (N): a waterfall.

Uruthuck (V): named after the headman of the local tribe. Now Milton.

Uyarrin (W): cleared ground.

W

Waarrar (Q): a river.

Waawaarawaa (N): fresh water.

Wabalingo (Q): goodbye.

Wabba (V): a bronze-wing pigeon.

Wacknarungyuka (W): tree of curiosity.

Wagerbillartgaree (W): a place where an emu was caught in the fork of a tree.

Waggaling (W): a spring where snakes are plentiful.

Wagga Wagga (N): there are a number of explanations offered for this name: crows; the call of the crows; many crows; a sick or dying man staggering or reeling with exhaustion; to dance; to slide; to grind. It will be noticed that there is some affinity between the last four meanings.

Wagin (W): the place where emus came to drink.

Wagininup (W): a large swamp which provided plenty of food.

Wagnup (W): a large rock above a spring of water.

Wagonga (N): a place of stinging nettles.

Wagra (N): crows.

Wahgumpah (Q): a turkey.

Wahgunyah (N): from *wah*, crows; *gunyah*, a shelter; the crows' resting place; beware!

Wahlooga (N): where are you going?

Wahpunyah (S): from *wahgunyah*, q.v.

Wahratta (N): a camping place.

Wahroonga (N): my home; our home.

Waikerie (S): wings, or anything that flies. It was a favourite resort for wildfowl.

Waitara (N): not an Aboriginal name, but an importation from New Zealand. Waitara in Taranaki probably came from *wai*, water; *tara* (short for *taranga*), wide steps. The story is that the Maori explorer Turi forded the river many hundreds of years ago with great strides; again, it is said that it means simply mountain peak, *tara* meaning peak. Again there is a legend that a young man set out in search of his father by successive throwings of his dart (*whai*, to follow; *tara*, dart). There is another Waitara on the Mohaka River which was so named because a Maori took with him the bones of his slave to scrape them and fashion them into spears (*tara*).

Wakothunta (V): a place of crows.

Walabah (N): needlewood tree.

Walcha (N): the sun.

Walgeemarrbimcaring (W): a place where crows stole the meat and carried it away.

Walgett (N): meeting of the waters; a river crossing; a long water hole.

Walginup (W): a swamp.

Walgooan (N): a high wind.

Walkeroon (N): a hanging vine to climb with. Now Amoefield.

Walkininnup or **Walkinup** (W): to rest a while.

Wallabadah (N): a stone.

Wallah (N): from *walla*, rain.

Wallanbillan (N): from *wallunbillung*, a stupid person. see *Wallenbillan*.

Wallangarrg (N): from *wallan*, water; *garra*, long: long water. There was a long lagoon at this place.

Wallarobba (N): gully with a plenteous rainfall.

Wallaroo (N and S): from *wadlawaru*, which was distorted to *wallawaroo*, and then took its final form. It means either a black mountain wallaby or a large brown kangaroo.

Wallatappe (N): three large water holes.

Walla Walla (N): plenty of rain.

Wallendbeen (N): a stony place; a stony hill.

Wallenbillan (N): from *wullungbullung*, a stupid or foolish person; a dance.

Wallerawa (N): men quarrelling and then departing.

Wallerawang (N): plenty of water.

Wallinuninnie (N): gravel.

Wallon (N): hot.

Walloo (Q): a snapper.

Walloway (S): a plain with plenty of wild turkeys.

Wallumburrawang (N): plenty of small white stones.

Wallunwong (N): give me a drink; stones.

Wallungbogal (N): a rock jutting out.

Walmer Walmer (W): literally carry carry; probably to carry a heavy load, or to carry many loads.

Wambangalong or **Wambanga-lang** (N): from *ouimboinga-line* or *wamboingoolah*, a mob of kangaroos; place for kangaroos.

Wambidgee (N): a man.

Wamboingoolian (N): from *wamboin*, a kangaroo; *goolian*, wish I had him! — a cry from the heart.

Wambool (N): a river.

Wamboyne (N): a kangaroo; a red kangaroo.

Wanalling (W): to die.

Wanbi (S): a dingo.

Wanbobra or **Wanbabra** (N): the head.

Wanboo (Q): devil-devil.

Wandalwallah (W): a burial ground.

Wandanandong or **Wandoo-wandong** (N): from *wunda wunda*, spirits who persecute the souls of the dead in an underworld.

Wandandian or **Wandiwandian** (N): the home of the lost lovers; a tribal name.

Wandearah (S): from *wandeahra*, big trees.

Wandella (N): from *wandellow*,

bark stripped from trees.
Large sheets of bark were
used for making temporary
huts and canoes, smaller ones
for carrying vessels.

Wandilo (S): a swamp where
there are native companions.

Wandinyallock, Wardiyallock,
or **Worriyallock** (V): running
water.

Wandiwandian or **Wandra-
wandian** (N): see *Wandandian*.

Wandong (N): spoiled timber.

Wandoowandong (N): the Evil
Spirit.

Wanerrah (W): a woman's
throwing stick. Women
usually carried a digging
stick, while the throwing
stick used in hunting was a
man's weapon.

Wanga (Q): a madman.

Wangam (Q): deaf.

Wangarange (Q): a lizard.

Wangaratta (V): nesting place
of shags; meeting of the
waters.

Wangary, Lake (S): from
wangaree, crows; or from
wangara, talk.

Wangdagup (W): floating reeds.

Wangianna (S): hill on a plain.

Wangi Wangi (N): night owl;
big water; an evergreen tree.

Wangoola (N): to dig.

Wangrah (N): a valley between
the mountains.

Wangun (Q): old man wallaby.

Wangurra (N): sleeping.

Waniguday (N): don't want it.

Wanmering (W): river died out.

Wantabadgery (N): a fighting
place.

Wantigong (V): a magpie.

Wappila (Q): a place where
there is a cave.

Waranalin (W): moving kangaroos.

Waratah (N and T): the well-
known red-flowering tree,
which was abundant in this
locality.

Warathar (N): wait for me.

Warawitcha (N): where land in
the river nearly forms an
island.

Warawollung (N): from *wol-
lung*, head. A high mountain
to the west of Lake Mac-
quarie was so named because
it bore a resemblance to a
human head.

Warbroon or **Warbro** (N): an
unexpected stopping place.
A journey was interrupted
here for some unexpected
and now unknown reason,
resulting in a diversion to
another place and eventual
return to the starting point.

Warcowie (S): from *wara-
chiowie*, the crows' water
hole.

Wardiyallock (V): see *Wandin-
yallock*.

Wardone (W): a crow.

Wardulup (W): a forest of
karri trees.

Wardup (W): water all summer.
Wareelahcohgarra (N): the land where the sun rises.
Waregong (W): black crows.
Wargambegal (N): crow come along.
Wargin (N): a crow.
Warialda (N): possibly from *worralda*, a place of wild honey.
Warilimericket (N): a cave under a mountain.
Warnagoon (V): native bear.
Warooka (S): a parrot with beautiful feathers.
Warracknabeal (V): flooded gum trees; large gum trees.
Warragai (N): plenty of sand.
Warragul (V): wild.
Warrah (N): falling rain.
Warrah (W): garments.
Warral (N): honey; honey bee.
Warramagullion (N): dogs fighting.
Warrambool (N): stream with banks overgrown with grass.
Warrambucca (N): a warm place.
Warrangle (V): a dingo; wild men.
Warrangong (N): a small berry-bearing tree.
Warrangunnia (N): a hole in the earth.
Warrapanillamullolacoopalline (N): a water hole with cane grass, shaped like a man's leg, with trees growing round about.

Warra Warra (Q): a fence.
Warrawarratinna (N): club foot; toes turned in.
Warrawee (N): come here; rest a while. This was a favourite resting place when on walk-about.
Warren (N): from *wurren* or *wurrena*, a large root. Other meanings: level; flat; strong.
Warrichatta (Q): a place where sharks are found.
Warrigal (N): from *warrgal*, a dingo.
Warrigal (Q): wild tribes and outlawed Aborigines, and especially wild dogs or dingoes. There were many wild dingoes, and while they were seldom domesticated, they were frequently used for hunting.
Warrigundi (N): a place of crows.
Warrimoo (N): an eagle.
Warrina (S): a place of rest. However it has also been stated that this is not an Aboriginal name, but was derived from Thomas Warriner who was in Babbage's journey of exploration in 1858.
Warringah (N): sign of rain.
Warringiddy (N): sweetheart.
Warriparri (S): a creek fringed with trees. Now Sturt River.
Warrnambool (V): a place of plenty; a grassy watercourse;

running swamps.

Warroo (N): a place of red hornets.

Warroul (Q): bees' nests.

Warrumbüngle Range (N): small mountains; short mountains.

Warrungen (N): a boomerang.

Washimberribin (N): a flying squirrel. Now Fairfield.

Watabora (N): a crow.

Watcham (V): a country where wild hops grow.

Wattah (N): a place of fire.

Wattamolla (N): a place near to running water.

Wauraltee (S): from *waural*, bandicoot; *tee*, an island. The bandicoots were plentiful on an island about three miles from the coast, and hunters swam across to it.

Waurdang (N): spoiled timber. The name commemorates an occasion when an Aboriginal was working at some article and spoiled it.

Waurdong (N): the home of the devil.

Wayandah (Q): a horse.

Wean (N): fire.

Weddin (N): to stay. Young men about to undergo the initiation tests were required to wait at this place before the ceremonies began.

Wee (N): a place of fire; wood. The word is part of a number of place names in New South Wales, and usually means fire, or has some connection with fire.

Weeamara or **Weeamera** (N): music.

Weeche (W): an emu.

Weedlealby (W): a place where powder, called *wilgy*, is obtained for painting the body prior to going into battle.

Weegerak (N): from *weogelah*, a resting place.

Weegoolgurra (N): a place of hot weather.

Weelu or **Weelia** (W): a shell.

Weemilah (N): a good view.

Weemobah (N): a place of fire; a place of permanent fire.

Weenga (N): to rest.

Weeraman (N): to play.

Weetaliba or **Weetalabah** (N): a place where the fire went out; a place where firewood was scarce.

Weewaa (N): fire thrown away.

Weighknarlbup (W): emu lost feathers.

Weja (N): to love.

Welcha (W): an eagle-hawk.

Welgalling (W): two large springs beside a hill.

Wemgowaa (N): a round hill.

Wendo (W): a white gum tree.

Werai (N): look out! An ingenious explanation is offered by the fact that Werai is a network of creeks, and that in the case of a sudden flood the cry will rise, "Look out!"

Werang (V): a place of spoon-bill ducks.

Wercan (Q): plenty of lilies.

Werigal (N): a dingo.

Werthelwa (N): a place where animals lick the ground.

Wharkuroogma (Q): a big water hole with plenty of ducks.

Wharthum (Q): plenty of water here.

Whian Whian (N): a tree with large roots; a large tree with a number of spears.

Whiporie (N): fine.

Whippengong (V): a magpie.

Whriba (Q): stone for making axes. Now South Molle (Great Barrier Reef).

Whyalla (S): a place of water.

Whyneema (W): women's spears.

Wiangarie (N): a pine ridge.

Wiberigan (N): a rainbow.

Widgelli (N): to drink.

Widgiewas (N): what do you want?

Wilbriggie (N): native mistletoe.

Wilcan (N): a gap through which the water flows in time of flood.

Wilcannia (N): a dingo; a gap through which water flows.

Wilga (N): hot.

Wilganbala (N): kicked in the eye.

Wilgarning (W): resting place for parrots.

Wilgerup (W): red ground.

Wilgo (N): from *willagoo* or *willgoo*, a swamp reed.

Wilgoyne (W): a water hole in the sand.

Wilkawatt (S): a dingo. Formerly called Cotton.

Willakulin (W): red clay land.

Willamalong (N): a sick man. An Aboriginal here contracted sickness which caused severe vomiting.

Willamulka (S): shining green stones.

Willandra (N): little waters; a creek.

Willeyganalgee (N): a place where possums are captured by smoking them out of their holes in hollow trees.

Willicking (W): a red hill.

Willieploma (N): a large possum.

Williewarrina (N): a possum standing up.

Willi Willi (N): possum in the bush.

Willochra (S): a flooded creek where polygonum bushes grow.

Willoring (N): honey running out of a tree; strained honey. Bees' honey was usually taken from holes in trees and eaten complete with its complement of insects, twigs, pieces of bark, and other impurities.

Willowie (S): a place of green

trees. This name was applied to Mount Remarkable when it was seen from a distance.

Willunga (S): from *willngga*, a place of green trees.

Willyama (N): a hill with a broken contour. It was originally intended that this should be the official name of Broken Hill, but eventually it was discarded.

Willyoogup (W): a spring of water.

Wilpenapound (S): a place of bent fingers.

Wiluna (W): from *weeloona*, the name being given because the bush curlew *weeloo* was frequently heard in the vicinity of the lake. Now Lake Violet.

Wimmera (V): a variant of *woomera*, the throwing stick used in hunting.

Winangubba (N): where a dingo stole meat.

Wincey (Q): the east wind.

Windaaning (W): a broken spear.

Windang (N): the scene of a fight.

Winderlup (W): a permanent creek.

Windgidgeon (N): burnt out.

Windjo (Q): a mountain kangaroo.

Wingadee (N): look at the big fire.

Wingello (N): to burn; burning.

Wingen (N): fire. Smoke has been seen to rise from fissures on the slopes of Mount Wingen.

Winninnie (S): many; a meeting place of the clans.

Winnunga (N): small.

Wiragulla (N): a parrot.

Wirega (N): clear ground.

Wirha (S): a species of acacia.

Wirmalngrang (S): the cave of the mopoke. Now Beachport.

Wirrabara (S): from *wirrabirra*, forest of gum trees and running water.

Wirrabilla (N): from *wirra*, teeth; *billa*, water; literally water with teeth in it. The water hole was supposed to be frequented by a devil fish.

Wirrah (N): tooth; teeth.

Wirramatya (S): gum tree flat. Now Laura.

Wirraminna (S): gum tree water.

Wirrarie (Q): rocks in a water hole.

Wirrasupenee (N): a place where kangaroos sleep.

Wirrawilla (S): green trees.

Wirreanda (S): from *wirraando*, a rock wallaby gum tree, i.e. a hollow tree where a wallaby was hiding.

Wirrega (S): people who live in the open forest.

Wirringerand (N): a bower bird.

Wirrinya (N): sleep.

Witgweri (V): wind whistling through the she-oaks.

Withamango (Q): to laugh.

Woakwine (S): my arm.

Wobbumarjoo (Q): clay which turns to bog in wet weather. Now Beenleigh.

Wocha (Q): a place of crocodiles.

Wodonga (V): an edible nut.

Wodrabiggunni (N): no-good fellow addicted to swearing.

Wogalup (W): a large carpet snake.

Woginorah (N): a dingo.

Wogle (N): one-eye. This point of land was named because of a one-eyed man who lived there. Now Tom Ugly's Point.

Wogoni (N): a codfish.

Wollar (N): a small flat by a creek.

Wollithiga (V): from *wolla*, water. It was possibly the original Aboriginal name for *Echuca*, q.v.

Wollomai (N): from *wollumii*, look round you; keep your eyes open, or look out!

Wollombi (N): meeting of the waters.

Wollomi (N): a snapper. Now Snapper Point.

Wollondilly River (N): water trickling over the rocks.

Wollongbar (N): a hole in the ground.

Wollongong (N): there are several explanations for the name, as follows; from *woolyunyah*, five islands; hard ground near the water; see, the monster comes! The latter was supposed to be an exclamation of fear uttered when the Aborigines saw a ship in full sail for the first time. It was pronounced *nwoolyarngungli*.

Wollumbin (N): a high mountain.

Wollun (N): hard ground.

Wolumla (N): a big water hole.

Wolwollin (W): a place where water runs over the rocks.

Wombarra (N): a black duck.

Wombat (N): the name of the animal.

Wombeyan (N): caves in the hills; a gigantic water rat.

Wombiana (N): kangaroos.

Wombinebong (N): a place where kangaroos feed.

Womboyne (N): big brown kangaroo; male kangaroo; that kangaroo; wombat hole.

Womerah (V): a *woomera* or throwing stick.

Womiulie (Q): sandhill snakes.

Wompah (N): debris from flood waters.

Wonaminka (N): plenty of boomerangs.

Wonawotha (Q): I don't know.

Wondecla (Q): meeting of the waters. Formerly called Nigger Creek.

Wondergetup (W): a tree.

Wondup (W): soft green moss on the water.

Wonga (Q): a native pigeon.

Wongahgah or **Wongigam** (N): a tallow wood tree.

Wongal (Q): a boomerang.

Wongalpong (Q): deaf.

Wongayerio (S): overwhelming water where the sun sinks. Now St Vincent's Gulf.

Wonghi (N): no.

Wongoni (N): a codfish.

Wong Wong (Q): a crow.

Wongyarra (S): one big hill. The name by which Mount Remarkable was known to the Aborigines when seen from close at hand. From a distance it was known as *Willowie*.

Wongybill (N): a place infested with ants' nests.

Wonogarup (W): a place of fat kangaroos.

Wonthaggi (V): to pull; drag; borne.

Woodenbalup (W): a good spring of water.

Woodenbong (N): a lagoon.

Woodrabeeka (N): no-good fellow.

Woodraliggunnie (N): no-good fellow who swears.

Woogaroo (Q): a whirlwind; a whirlpool.

Woolami (N): a good place for catching snapper.

Woolark (W): a black cockatoo with a white tail.

Wooleringup (W): plenty of dingoes.

Wooli (N): a cedar tree.

Woolkabunning (W): you have been here and gone away again.

Woollahra (N): a look-out.

Woolloomooloo (N): there are several explanations: from *wullaoomullah*, a young kangaroo; whirling round; and, in connection with the latter meaning an attempt by Aborigines to pronounce the word windmill.

Woolloowin (Q): fish.

Woologallar (Q): an elopement.

Woolooncappeman (Q): from *wooloon*, whirling; *cappeman*, water: whirling water; whirlpool.

Wooloongabba (Q): whirling round.

Wooloongarra (Q): a large rock.

Woolowa (N): a muddy flat.

Woolrabunning (W): you have been here and have gone again.

Woolway (N): from *wullwye*, a sheltered place.

Woomang (Q): a little fish.

Woomera (S): a throwing stick.

Woonarne (W): a wild duck.

Woongarra (N): a camp.

Woongarra (Q): a brigalow tree.

Wooningcanning (W): where wild ducks flock and play together.

Woonona (N): from *wunona*, to sleep; a place of young wallabies.

Wooroongarry (Q): a vine used as a rope for climbing trees.

Woorroowoolgan (W): a bend in the river; a lagoon where waterfowl are plentiful.

Wootheroo (W): seaweed.

Woram (N): a left-handed man.

Wordonguttergin (W): a spring close to a large rock beside a hill.

Worgan (N): a crow.

Worije (W): a river.

Woringerong (N): from *derong derong*, a storm bird.

Woronora (N): a black rock.

Worragalla (N): a dingo crossing a stream.

Worriyallock (V): see *Wandin-yallock*.

Wowine (W): similar; alike.

Woy Woy (N): deep water; a lagoon; a porpoise.

Wraaha (Q): a dead bloodwood tree.

Wubbera (N): small stones.

Wudina (S): granite rocks.

Wudjongmoorjung (N): grass. Now Busby's Flat.

Wullinga (Q): a black duck.

Wullwunthar (N): very crooked. Now Dignam's Creek.

Wumbulgal (N): a black duck.

Wunnamurra (N): an eagle-hawk.

Wunnuckin (V): named after the headman of the local tribe. Now Hamilton.

Wurrawana (T): haunted.

Wurrole (Q): heart.

Wyadbena (N): from *wianbean*, a creek of running water.

Wyalga (Q): plenty of kangaroo rats.

Wyan (N): the roots of a tree.

Wyanga (N): mother.

Wybalena (N): man sit down here.

Wyee (N): fire.

Wyengoo (Q): where are you going?

Wynarka (S): a stranger.

Wynnum (Q): a breadfruit tree.

Wyong (N): from *woy*, water; **W***ong*, a spring or place of a spring: a place of running water; a place where Christmas bells grow.

yuna (V): clear water.

Y

Yaamba (Q): a camping ground.

Yabboine (Q): sister.

Yabbra (N): a runaway, or outlaw; also a large bush.

Yacka (S): from *yackamoorundie*, sister to the big river.

Yackendahwirin (N): a turtle resting on the water.

Yackiel (Q): a bandicoot.

Yagobie (N): a big river.

Yagoona (N): today.

Yahwang (Q): a hornet.

Yahwulpa (Q): a wasp.

Yalata (S): a shellfish. Now

Fowler's Bay.

Yalla (N): go away quickly.

Yallakool (N): clear water.

Yallaroi (N): stony; white flint found here; possibly a tribal name.

Yallatup (W): a good place for tea-tree.

Yalleroi (Q): a lagoon.

Yallumarina (Q): plenty of boxwood.

Yalumba (S): all the country round about.

Yamadagoolburra (N): I understand you.

Yamagulli (N): signs of water.

Yamba (N): a headland.

Yamble (N): laughing; playing; joking.

Yampi Sound (W): from *yampee*, fresh water.

Yanagin (W): green trees growing here.

Yanbulla (N): two strangers.

Yanco (N): running water; the song of running water.

Yandembah (N): the home of ghosts.

Yanderrah (N): a turpentine tree.

Yandiah (S): a camp where there is lively gossip.

Yandina (Q): a walk, path, or road; a little place for water.

Yangalla (Q): sit down.

Yaraka (Q): an unmarried man.

Yarardup (W): plenty of dry wood.

Yararley (N): a white man.

Yararleymerrigi (N): a white woman.

Yarcowie (S): wide water. The name was given by Governor Musgrave in 1874.

Yareing (W): high up.

Yarra River (V): a word in common use in Victoria, *yarra* usually refers to running water. Other meanings given are: swift motion; a hiding place; a red gum tree.

Yarrahapinni, Yareehappinni or **Yarrihapini** (N): a native bear rolling down hill; the head of a native bear rolling down the hill.

Yarraking (W): to run; to go quickly.

Yarraldool (N): small stones.

Yarram (V): from *yarrem yarrem*, plenty of water; waterfalls.

Yarramalong (N): a place of wild horses.

Yarraman (Q): a horse; a plain; a tooth.

Yarramar (N): to swim.

Yarrangobilly (N): a flowing stream.

Yarrawonga (V): where the shags build their nests; where the wonga pigeons are found.

Yarra Yarra (V): ever-flowing river.

Yarrimup (W): a hill.

Yarrunga (N): large trees.

Yarruppe (N): a gum tree.

Yarryn (N): whiskers.

Yass (N): probably from *yarh* or *yahr*, both forms of *yarra*, q.v., meaning running water. Another theory is that the name comes from *yarratahr*, with the same meaning. There is a story which is almost certain to be apochryphal, that when Hume asked an Aboriginal to report on the country ahead and to tell him whether it was good, the man replied, "Ya-ass, plains." And so the name Yass came into being.

Yatala (Q): flooded. The original name of this place was *Woogoomarjee*, but it was renamed by Arthur Dixon after *Yatala* in South Australia.

Yatala (S): flooded.

Yathong (N): large sandhills.

Yatteyatah (N): a double waterfall.

Yeerongpilly (Q): a sandy gully.

Yelarbon (Q): a water lily which grows in a lagoon. Formerly known as The Desert.

Yelgecup (W): a place where kangaroos lie down.

Yelgun (N): the sun.

Yellanjurong (Q): plenty of food.

Yellebelling (W): saltwater pool.

Yelleyellup (W): a freshwater spring.

Yelta (S): a small animal.

Yeltukka (S): a new place.

Yengarie (Q): a sleepy place.

Yeolangs (V): a black cockatoo with a red tail.

Yeo Yeo (N): a devil-devil.

Yeraan (N): a high wind.

Yeraberi (Q): a flat-topped mountain.

Yeran (Q): a girl.

Yeraran (N): a whip snake.

Yerdanup (W): a blackboy thicket.

Yerdine (W): a semi-circular hill.

Yerin (V): from *yeriong* or *yerung*, a place where boys had a front tooth knocked out during the initiation rites.

Yerinandah (N): kill and eat.

Yerong (N): see *Yerin*.

Yerrah (N): to dig up some buried object. At this beach in Botany Bay a number of articles had been buried in the sand for safety.

Yerrantaccu (Q): plenty of cattle here.

Yerriebah (Q): come this way.

Yerrinan (N): a large gum tree.

Yerrinbool (N): a wood duck.

Yerrine (W): a root.

Yerringhe (N): a water wagtail.

Yerroulbine (N): swiftly running water. Now Longnose Point.

Yeryeri (W): plenty of water.

Yethera (N): three roads; three tracks.

Yeulup (W): a place where

kangaroos lie down in the dust.

Yhetlanardung or **Yhtlanet** (W): a breeding place for fantails.

Yiddah (N): to recover from sickness.

Yilgarn (W): white quartz.

Yilvung (Q): a mocking bird.

Yinnell (Q): a creek.

Yoganup (W): a spring.

Yokanup (W): plenty of dingoes.

Yokine (W): a dingo.

Yongerlocelkucup (W): a plain where the kangaroos dance.

Yongermoranelyeirup (W): a place where kangaroos scratch holes in the ground.

Yongurra (N): a goanna.

Yoogali (N): to rejoice; to exult.

Yoolarai (N): the name of the local tribe.

Yoongarilup (W): a place where kangaroos scratch holes in the ground.

Yoorooga (N): my home.

Yooth (Q): a sand drift.

Yooyoongan (Q): a whale.

Youcoora (W): a kangaroo.

Younda Younda (N): a sheet of bark.

Youndoogeedan (N): rocks where stone axes are sharpened.

Youring (W): a waterless plain.

Yourol (Q): a whip snake.

Yowangup (W): plenty of yams.

Yueagie (W): poor; miserable.

Yukieyackine (W): near a lake.

Yulbieyulbiebundilla (N): box trees with *yulbie* berries growing amongst them.

Yulgilbar or **Yulgibar** (N): a big log; a thin piece of wood.

Yullundry (N): green wattle trees.

Yuluma (N): a wallaroo.

Yumbuck (W): a paperbark tree.

Yumbunga (N): a camp.

Yunderup (W): a place for water.

Yungaburra (Q): a place haunted by spirits. Originally *Alumba* but subsequently changed to *Yungaburra* to avoid confusion with *Aloomba*.

Yungarup (W): hills by the sea.

Yunta (S): this has been modestly defined as "referring to a woman's anatomy".

Yuragga (Q): a place where plenty of feathers are found.

Yuraraba (Q): a round mountain.

Yureidla (S): place of the ears. Now Mount Lofty. See also *Uraidla*.

Yurgo (S): a long way.

Yurrah (Q): plenty of trees.

Z

Zach (Q): hungry.

APPENDIX A
WORD LIST

Note: Fuller descriptions of many of the words in this list will be given under the appropriate entry in the main contents of the book.

A

Acacia: *Namoi; Wirha.
Alike: Wowine.
Always There: Killara.
Ambush: Jerrungarugh.
Anger: Colah.
  angry: Coolah.
  angry rainbow: Teerawah.
Animal:
  licking ground: Werthelwa.
  liver: Thabbat.
  small: Yelta.
Ankle:
  shapely: Booyamurra.
Ants:
  big white: Ironmongie.
  greenhead: Chilgerrie; Moonbil.
  hill: Burra.
  jumper: Durranbah; Turranbar.
  little, reply to: Dunowie.
  nest: Mungahwakaah; Purribangla; Wongybill.
  plenty of: Mingajibbi.
  red: Kingaroy.
  red, nests of: Carrarthang.
  small black: Teta.
  tunnelling: Burgooney.

*Acacia is the generic name of the wattle, q.v., of which there are many species. The North American black locust tree is often called the false acacia.

white: Eragorara.
white, nest of: Keirbarban.
Apple Tree: Boiboigar; Kundabung.
  sap: Malaria.
Arm: Guine.
  my: Woakwine.
Ashes: Boobijan.
  flying through the air: Tonderbruine.
  like sawdust: Donnabewong.
Axe: Balonne; Congha; Mogil; Thingabargan.
  rocks for sharpening: Trungley; Youndoogeedan.
  stone for making: Larow; Mogil Mogil; Morgyup; Whriba.

B

Baby: Canbo; Chargem; Kiandool; Tatham.
  boy: Coombah.
Back:
  man or animal: Bulkirra.
Backbone: Carmumdagual.
Bad: Gootoo.
  people: Musero.
  temper: Coolah.
  very: Ingildo.
Bags:
  for drums: Booningi.
Bait: Jerbam.

Bandicoot: Burraga; Cooyong;
　　Tagboin; Yackiel.
　island of: Wauraltee.
　plenty of: Toora.
Banks of Stream:
　grassy: Warrambool.
　red: Goyda; Koolunga.
Bare:
　hill: Jindalee; Nariah.
　place: Narriah.
Bark: Bulong; Currunghi;
　　Cussrunghi; Dungay; Pika-
　　pene; Tollerin; Wandella;
　　Younda Younda.
　dents: Goondi.
　like death adder: Tomingley.
　tea-tree: Nambour.
Barnacles: Korogaro.
Bartering of Women: Hen-
　nendri.
Basin in Hills: Uralba.
Bathing Place: Coalbaggie;
　　Kieinde.
Battle: Caloola; Sauming.
Beach:
　long: Uringa.
　long sandy: Kiyung.
　sandy: Bangalee; Cronulla;
　　Gunnamatta; Mortalup.
　stones on: Karrara.
Bear, Native (Koala): Banga-
　　roo; Coolac; Jular; Koole-
　　wong; Nargoon; Pucawan.
　large: Coolawin.
　rolling down hill: Yarraha-
　　pinni.
Beard: Ungar.
Beautiful: Bega; Boogo Boogo;
　　Nunkeri; Tarebarre.

country: Tathra.
girl: Minil; Moogal.
ground: Terrabulla.
place: Illowra; Kiah.
view: Taronga Park.
woman: Merinda.
Bed of River: Kalpara.
Beech Tree: Binnaburra;
　　Coolowyn; Mumblebone.
Beef: Dinga; Tingha.
　plenty of: Moolabulla.
Bees: Gurana; Warral.
　nest of: Mahyl; Medulegah;
　　Warroul.
Beetle: Moogoon.
　floating on whirlpool: Tonga-
　　robin.
　purple: Nyngan.
Beetwood Tree: Mumblebone.
Behind, Long Way: Naraman.
Bellbird: Bean Bean; Punt-
　　puntpundaloo.
Belly: Binge.
　big: Booreebiddy.
　lie down on: Tamalee.
　river, shape of: Coblinine.
Bend in River: Bungleboori;
　　Miandetta; Tarcoola;
　　Thelim; Ulmarra; Woorroo-
　　woolgan.
Bent Fingers: Wilpenapound.
Berries: Nardu; Nerrigundah.
　good: Patchiewarra.
　yulbie: Yulbieyulbiebundilla.
Better: Maramba.
Between: Gingham.
Beware: Wahgunyah.
Big: Booral.
Birds: Boun; Gymea.

extinct: Tootool.
place of: Bibbenluke; Bimbi.
place of little: Terrigal.
plenty of: Birdup; Goodie
Goodie.
plenty of birds sit down:
Carawah.
plenty of green: Jeggibil.
plenty of moojung: Mooje-
bing.
plenty of small: Booyah;
Buthia Buthia.
song: Booyah.
Birthplace:
of child: Goonian.
of king: Bogan Gate.
Bitten by Snake: Turron-
gouuddi.
Bitter Swamp: Burraga.
Bittern: Poonboon.
Black: Narra-.
Blackboy:
stick: Marbolup.
thicket: Ingenup; Yerdanup.
Blackbutt Tree: Goolarabang.
Blackfish: Kooweerup.
Blankets: Cambee.
Bleeding:
hands: Murragoedgoen.
nose: Merrygoen.
Blind: Goonoo; Mercadool;
Mooki; Tye.
Blood: Ballina; Coomera; Cul-
lengoin; Cummara.
Bloodwood Tree: Benowa;
Boonah; Groombunda;
Mingaletta.
dead: Wraaha.

Blowflies: Booungun; Burrimul;
Dewitt.
Boggy: Tantanoola.
Boiling Spring: Nelshaby.
Bones: Meriamunka; Moojoey;
Tubbul.
bony: Narromine.
in kangaroo's leg: Pulbging.
Boomerang: Burraganee;
Warrungen; Wimmera;
Wongal.
man holding: Bolaro; Bul-
gandry; Bulgandramine.
plenty: Wonaminka.
sword-like: Burringbar.
Borne: Wonthaggi.
Bottle Tree: Pinkee.
Bottle-brush Flower: Pendicup.
Boundary: Towri.
Bowels: Mooball.
Bower-bird: Wirringerand.
Box Tree: Coolabah; Kirip;
Uranquinty;Yulbieyulbie-
bundilla.
flooded: Booligal.
grey: Girral.
place of: Pyree.
plenty of: Yallumarina.
stump of: Merungora.
white-leaved: Bibil.
with mistletoe: Topiely.
yellow: Uardry.
Boy: Borup; Coedie; Yerin.
baby: Coombah.
playground of: Purryburry.
small: Tabboo; Thabbo.
Bramble: Koikalingba.
Branch: Nundryculling.
Bread: Moorine.

possum's: Ulamambri.

Breaking: Bungiebomah.

Bream: Bungulla.

Breast: Kooroomie; Manaro; Monaro; Mudah; Namoi; Nea.

broken, of emu: Timbrebongey.

to breast: Bringagee.

Breathing: Tippoorarie.

Breeding Place:

fantails': Yhetlanardung.

Brigalow Tree: Burradoo; Woongarra.

Bringing: Tycannah.

Broken: Banda Banda.

hand: Marrapigup.

limb: Bunglegumbie.

ribs: Gnurrlarkendockenarup.

spears: Geetchboordankendoo; Gutchboordankendockenarup; Windaaning.

stone: Turrabirren.

thigh: Terramungamine.

tree: Dilga.

Brother: Kulde; Nackara, Nooan.

Bubble: Nerbichup.

Budda Tree: Budda.

Bulb: Curtmerup.

Bullfrog: Bullakibil; Gooloorooeybri.

Bullock: Boolbilly; Coonamble; Jabuk.

Bulrush: Mungungboora.

swamp: Cambalup.

Bunyip: Cooraburrama.

Burial Ground: Bergalin; Bin-

nawan; Naratoola; Wandalwallah.

Burning, Burnt: Windgidgeon; Wingello.

earth: Tubbo.

grass: Gidgaween; Kullateenee.

log: Marradong; Ulandi.

man: Cockelup.

trees: Moorombunnia.

Bush, Bushes: Berri; Earea; Mecrano; Yabbra.

fire: Cubaway; Kallulahwon; Keedirah; Kimbah; Narrie.

plain: Boorthanna.

Butterfly: Naliandrah.

Buttocks: Mernmerna.

By-and-by: Uralla.

C

Cabbage Palm: Dundilkar; Mollon; Tongarra.

Calf: Catherko.

Camp and **Camping Places:** Baagna; Ballarat; Brewongle; Goondi; Garema; Goudjoulgang; Gun-; Kooroora; Kywung; Maggea; Marnyong; Miamia; Minemoorong; Mongarumba; Murwillumbah; Nadda; Nerrigundah; Noora; Quamby; Toowacka; Wahratta; Woongarra; Yaamba; Yumbunga.

abandoned: Boolbadah; Eragorara; Umpiebong.

big: Bega; Jumberdine.
by the river: Tumut
by the sea: Elanora.
fire: Kallgallup.
good: Carkginginup: Elou-
era; Gerrut; Quabin.
hunting: Turramboyne.
in the hills: Goorack
Goorack.
of lively gossip: Yandiah.
of the moon: Keewong.
parrots': Parraweena.
poor: Grong Grong.
stinking: Eurabuga.
tonight: Gibba.
white man's: Apurlu; Man-
tung.
winter: Karoonda.
Cane: Migeengum.
Canoe: Bermagui; Eurobodalla;
Gogeldrie; Koonadan.
two: Murrumburrah.
Carrot: Kundle Kundle; Kurnel.
Carrying: Narromine; Walmer
Walmer.
Cascade: Galliebarinda.
Cat: Punchumgum.
Cat Bird: Jiggi.
Catching:
man: Dunnangmumma.
possums: Willeyganalgee.
Cattle: Bullockina; Yerrantaccu.
Caught:
by the head: Cobbadamana.
dingoes: Turrumga.
emu: Wagerbillartgaree.
Cave: Benomera; Carramolane;
Pirrin; Wappila; Warili-

mericket; Wombeyan.
of mopoke: Wirmalngrang.
of a spirit: Nargan.
path to the: Nangwarry.
Cedar Tree: Wooli.
red: Manimoril.
Centipede: Meinya.
Ceremony: see also *Initiation*.
Kuburra; Nocuting; Ourim-
bah.
Cherry Tree: Moombarriga.
Child and **Children:** Boobajool;
Chargin; Nubba.
born here: Goonian.
crying: Ewmbunlie.
died here: Gunyan.
tossed up in arms: Bodalla.
Chinaman: Onua.
Chip: Kindee.
Choking: Cronulla.
Chopping: Bungega.
Christmas Bells: Wyong.
Clay: Booleroo; Mungery;
Tumpoaba; Wobbumar-
joo.
coloured: Mirrool.
red: Cobar; Coochimudlo;
Coodging; Cudgegong;
Cudgen; Mungeribah; ·
Willakulin.
white: Illawarra.
Clear Ground: Uyarrin;
Wirlga.
Clear Water: Wyuna; Yalla-
kool.
Cliff: Tamplagooda.
Clinging: Nubhoygum.
Cloak:
kangaroo skin: Berangin.

possum skin: Bunbibilla.
to sew a: Curbollie.
Close: Echunga.
Clouds: Chounboon.
Club: Kotara; Nulla Nulla.
Club Foot: Warrawarratinna.
Coal: Nikkinba.
Coast: Belardoo.
Cockatoo: Biloela.
  black: Beabula; Cererch;
    Durrebar; Nowra; Robin-
    dalgar; Woolark; Yeo-
    yangs.
  place of: Merrywinebone.
  plenty of: Marianbone.
  white: Guerie; Guyra; Ker-
    rick; Kiara; Monache;
    Umarri.
Cod: Hinnomunjie; Wogoni;
  Wongoni.
Cold: Gadara; Parilla; Tug-
  gerah.
  a: Curra.
  place: Iggin; Mulgarnup.
  plain: Tuggernong.
  weather: Bookra; Kallaroo.
Collar-bone: Tanbil.
Collecting: Kunghah.
Come: Bah.
  here: Warrawee.
  this way: Yerriebah.
Comet: Turaku.
Companion: Mittagong.
Company: Milperra.
Contempt, Expression of: Mila-
  munda.
Contented: Mudgee.
Cook, Captain: see Gerringong;
  Kundle Kundle; Kurnel.

Cooking: Bucking; Gammain.
Coolamon: Cargelligo; Coolamon; Tatuali.
Copper: Cobar.
Coral Tree: Goonellabah.
Corner: Longorong; Nunnook.
Corroboree: Bora; Goonegah;
  Kerrabee; Kijini; Knulgoweedie; Moronobin; Munayang.
Cotton Tree: Talwalpin.
Coughing: Goonoo Goonoo.
Country: Yalumba.
  beautiful: Tathra.
  between lake and sea: Bil-
    lenargil.
  enemies': Coomandook.
  good: Dandarragan; Tatia-
    ra.
  my: Bungaree; Nunyahboo-
    gera; Tabulam.
  open: Cooma.
  open grass: Tyagarah.
  poor: Boonoo Boonoo;
    Goonoo Goonoo.
  rough: Narraburra.
  wet: Nounmoning.
  what country do you come
    from: Tarregomoonbung-
    goonine.
  where quandong grows: Ber-
    tical.
  where wild hops grow:
    Watcham.
  wild sandy: Balookyambut.
Cow: Cowabbie.
Crab: Chubie; Tabby Tabby.
Crab Fish: Nalloor.
Crane: Bookoor; Kououk.

Crater Lake: Barrine.
Crawling: Buckawackah; Duri.
Crayfish: Belleringah; Ingar; Morongla; Murrami; Nyngan.
Creek: Adelong; Adjungbilly; Anurie; Beetaloo; Belleringah; Billanbri; Billeroy; Bingarra; Bogobogalong; Bulla Bulla; Bung-; Bungonia; Bungoona; Collaroy; Cookamobila; Cooroombong; Dungatewakaah; Edgeroi; Gunning; Gurley; Kangiangi; Kooloobong; Lirambenda; Malaraway; Mookimawybra; Mungahwakaah; Nadjongbilla; Nerbichup; Nyngan; Orroroo; Pallal; Purpur; Queeryourga; Quipolly; Tillery; Tungbung; Warriparri; Wollar; Wyadbena; Yinnell.
  big: Bulladelah; Burren; Catthalalla; Gunyerwarildi; Warrabri.
  crooked: Bucca Bucca; Bundall; Kalybucca.
  flooded: Willochra.
  muddy: Tarparrie.
  of plenty: Kalachalpa.
  place of: Boggabri.
  right-hand: Tintenbar.
  saltwater: Kooparaback.
  singing: Eungai.
  small: Dobikin; Narang; Naranagi; Turramurra; Willandra.

Crocodile:
  big: Bedberry.
  in lagoon: Gongora.
  place of: Wocha.
  plenty of: Iarangutta.
Crooked: Wullwunthar.
  river: Nambucca.
  timber: Tomanbill.
  water: Kalybucca.
Crossing Place: Berriwerri; Bingeraba; Birribi; Dourim; Walgett.
  shallow: Tullalar.
Crow: Wagra; Wangary; Wardone; Wargin; Watabora; Wong Wong; Worgan.
  black: Waregong.
  call of: Wagga Wagga.
  come along: Wargambegal.
  nest: Cockamongar; Wahgunyah.
  place of: Tallagandra; Wakothunta; Warrigundi.
  place where meat carried away by: Walgeemarrbimcaring.
  walking: Thulley.
  water hole: Warcowie.
Crowd: Gillendoon.
Crying: Berringoo; Minyagoyugilla.
  child: Ewmbunlie.
Cuckoo: Murgah.
  note of: Toowong.
Curiosity, Tree of: Wacknarungyuka.
Curlew: Cooeeburra; Wiluna.
Cut and Cutting: Binya; Moopoo.

foot: Gygam.

grass: Murracompagoorandannie.

man: Coolyaganah.

sinew: Comarra.

tree: Galantapa.

with axe: Gundagai.

Cypress Pine: Chinchilla; Gooray.

D

Dance and **Dancing:** Dumbulli; Wagga Wagga; Wallenbillan.

kangaroos: Legerup; Yongerlocelkucup.

Dark and **Darkness:** Bullawie; Goodah; Narra-; Nooroo; Oomcurry.

side: Boolooinahl.

swamp: Mooroduc.

Daughter: Koorine.

Day: Coonbar.

Daylight: Kiwa.

Deaf: Barnawatha; Wangam; Wongalpong.

Death, Dead and **Dying:** Crumbana; Gobung; Koonthaparee; Kumal; Moochingoo; Moombooldool; Wanalling.

child: Gunyan.

dog: Moyekaeeta.

Death Adder: Bugilbone; Coondoo; Mooroobie; Tomingley.

Debris: Wompah.

Destitution: Gunida.

Devil Fish: Wirrabilla.

Devils: Comeacome; Quingun; Wandanandong; Wanboo; Yeo Yeo.

hill of: Gailagup.

place of: Merrygining; Waurdong.

plenty of: Chinocup; Mulcurriberry.

Diamond Sparrow: Edieowie.

Difficult: Moonan.

Digging: Carripan; Wangoola; Yerrah.

Digging Stick: Connay; Cuni.

Dilly Bag: Coolabulling; Dugandang; Thuntalbi.

reeds used to make them: Numira.

Dingo: Boorooma; Chatterup; Cudlee; Dingo; Euchie; Merri; Merri Merri; Mirribandini; Thurlgoona; Wanbi; Warrangle; Warrigal; Werigal; Wilcannia; Wilkawatt; Woginorah; Yokine.

caught: Turrumga.

crossing stream: Worragalla.

dead: Merribooka.

fighting: Warramagullion.

place of: Merrigang.

plenty of: Arowacka; Merribegia; Merrigal; Mittagong; Wooleringup; Yokanup.

stole meat: Winangubba.

tail: Coombullnee.

tracks: Calyeeeruka.

Dirt: Coonamble.

Dirty: Tobbery.
Distance: Bunora.
  short: Kielpa.
Distant: Garah; Goondi;
  Gundi; Indi; Narrawa; Nor-
  ring; Parairie.
Divorced: Myponga.
Dogwood Tree: Casino.
Dove: Kolodong; Towealgra.
  grey: Gooragoodoo.
  ground: Coorparoo.
  hawk: Gilyne.
Down of Eagle Hawk: Gowrie.
Dragging: Wonthaggi.
Draught: Gadara.
Drinking: Ettamogah; Nijong;
  Wallunwong; Widgelli.
  eagles: Cootapatamba;
  Koulabelamba.
  water: Coacatocalleen.
Drought: Eabungyalgo.
Drowning: Murragurra.
Drum: Booningi; Coombie.
Dry:
  grass: Boorlahboorloo.
  ground: Benhennie; Durran
  Durran; Uloom.
  spring: Killiting.
  time: Kunjara.
  wood: Yarardup.
Duck: Burrawang; Goondiwindi; Karangi; Woon-
  arne; Wooningcanning.
  black: Killowill; Mara;
  Moolpa; Wombarra; Wul-
  linga; Wumbulgal.
  musk: Benalla.
  plenty of: Arkarra; Wharkuroogma.

  spoonbill: Quingmory;
  Werang.
  whistling: Chipalee.
  white: Marama.
  wood: Eringanerin; Goonaroo; Yerrinbool.
Dumb: Barnawatha.
Dust: Goombaban; Murnal;
  Yeulup.

E

Eager: Kahibah.
Eagle: Warrimoo.
  down: Gowrie.
  drinking: Cootapatamba;
  Kootapatamba; Koulabe-
  lamba.
  nests: Boundahalcarra;
  Tobagangang.
Eagle-hawk: Mullion; Mungarry; Welcha; Wunna-
  murra.
  nest: Mulyanjandera.
  place of: Mulyan.
Ear: Deeragun; Kurri Kurri;
  Peedver; Uraidla; Yur-
  eidla.
  hair growing out of: Gooringaragunambone.
Earth: Thurgoona.
  burnt: Cobar; Tubbo.
  cracks in: Tugwantallaban.
  red: Guaballing; Kopurraba.
  rocky: Thurlgona.
Earthquake: Bussiwarrallwarrall.
East:
  looking: Croajingalong;

Nackara.

men of the: Krowathun-koolung.

wind: Wincey.

Eating: Ellengerah; Thallmoy; Yerinandah.

Echo: Gangalook; Myangup; Quidong.

Eclipse of Moon: Niangala.

Eel: Duelgum; Umboodee.

caught: Cussigungaringhi.

escaped: Turrumtalone.

sleep: Jerrara; Parramatta.

Eggs:

emu: Caltipurti.

hens': Howregan.

plenty of: Irkara.

yolk: Menindie.

Elbow: Coopernook; Goolwa.

Elder: Pinnaroo.

Elder Tree: Marlee.

Elopement: Woologallar.

Emu: Bunnacower; Coolberry; Cullya; Curramulka; Dangin; Dunwinnie; Kunanty; Owenyonni; Peddybang; Weeche.

breast of: Timbrebongey.

dead: Eurabuga.

droppings: Charra.

eggs: Caltipurti.

foot: Dennawan.

lost feathers: Weighknarlbup.

lying: Ooringuldain.

place of: Ngarronba; Toolijooa; Wagerbillartgaree; Wagin.

Enemies: Coomandook.

Entrance to Sea: Nambucca.

Estuary: Terranora.

Ever-flowing: Morialta; Yarra Yarra.

Evergreen: Kallioota; Wangi Wangi.

Evil Spirit: Boonboolong; Wandoowandong.

Eye: Koro; Melmel; Mil; Tibarri.

gone away: Milbong.

kicked in the: Wilganbala.

many: Millamurra; Milmil.

one: Wogle.

scum on the: Kouming.

sharp: Mailidup.

sore: Gundurimbah; Mildura; Milparinka.

spear in the: Millagun.

F

Falling: Gullingari; Tamplagooda.

Falling Star: Derrilin; Girilambone.

Fantail: Yhetlanardung.

Fat: Bulkee.

Father: Dwella; Myeah.

Fear, Expression of: Gerringong; Wollongong.

Feathers: Corama; Gundeerari; Minarcobrinni; Yuragga.

Feeding: Wombinebong.

Feet: Chinna; Jenolan; Jinna; Mundowery; Thinnungwille; Tidnacornarrinna.

bad: Jinnerbeeker.

big: Jinnerculurdy.

cut: Gygam.

Fence: Warra Warra.

Ferns: Boikonumba; Bunga-wahl; Coocarah; Coomera; Cowar; Culmara; Knameri-lup; Mayurra; Mulubinba.

Fern Root: Uki.

Fig Tree: Nabiac; Taree; Thurre; Tumbulgum.

Fight and **Fighting:** Alldalla; Badyeba; Ballina; Bullen Bullen; Bundi; Garoolgan; Pungonda.

dingoes: Warramagullion.

over women: Lridalah.

wombats: Mowbardonemar-godine.

Fighting Place: Goolahgelum; Kanimbla; Mororo; Wanta-badgery; Windang.

Fine: Whiporie.

Fine Weather: Jeedbowlee.

Finger: Maira; Merrgining; Wilpena Pound.

nail: Eulomogo.

Fire: Bibboorah; Boree; Cala-wathi; Cullanine; Culle-mine; Galgopin; Koroit; Mookimawybra; Wean; Wee; Weewaa; Wingen; Wyee.

camp: Kallgallup.

extinguished: Weetaliba.

from mountain: Cambe-warra.

look at the: Wingadee.

lucky fellow: Coolbaroo-mookoo.

place of: Calamia; Wattah; Weemobah.

woman by: Eenaweena.

Firewood: Calaberthaniga.

no: Moramana; Weetaliba.

First:

man: Kurri Kurri.

place: Marralmeedah.

Fish and **Fishing:** Andiah; Ball-ina; Gemalla; Mundoora; Neibichup; Ogeea; Pata-walonga; Piatarria; Pir-ralea; Quipolly; Tambo; Woolami; Woolloowin.

clean up: Bettuyungaany-sung.

die: Barringum.

plenty of: Howlong; Min-namurra; Quatquatta; Tabbigong.

small: Buljarngennee; Woo-mang.

stinging: Gruegarnie.

swimming: Queerbri.

Fish Eagle: Illowra.

Fishing Ground: Brewarrina; Goorawigah; Guyra; Mudieyarra; Noarlunga; Tugullinbah.

good: Kiama.

large: Bouderee.

woman's: Boorageree.

Fishing Line: Gillingkeleen.

Fishing Net: Nangarie.

Fish Spear: Kianga.

Five Finger: Murrarundi; Mur-rurundi.

Flame Tree: Bullawhay; Nam-bour.

Flat: Coatneal; Coomunderry; Cudal; Gugetup; Munna;

Tingha; Warren; Wollar; Woolowa.

gum tree: Wirramatya.

Flathead Fish: Cumbalum; Cumbulam.

Fleas: Bogong; Breeza; Edibegebege.

Flesh: Dadgra; Kudgeree.

Flies: Boolaroo; Junburra; Melnar.

anything that: Waikerie.

Flint: Koichgomorlgup; Tondaburine.

white: Madiwaitu; Yallaroi.

Flood: Boobigan; Dulgum; Moutaree; Mundoora; Thoowata; Wilcan; Wilcannia; Willochra; Yatala.

debris from: Wompah.

Flour: Chulora; Mulkblourway; Tarcutta.

bag: Puranga.

Flowers: Bootill; Coori; Girraween; Goorawin; Kawana.

blue: Marrangaroo.

bottle-brush: Pendicup.

kuruba: Kolorinbri.

mulga: Oodnadatta.

place of: Collarendebri.

red: Bintamiling.

waratah: Waratah.

wattle: Barreenong.

white: Chittennup; Minore.

Flowing: Gil Gil.

Flying Fox and **Squirrel:** Bungobaine; Washimberribin.

gully: Jebropilly.

plenty of: Bumgobittah; Bungawitta; Iargarong.

wing of: Currimundri.

Foam: Gingie.

Fog: Curroon.

Food: Mutooroo; Yellanjurong.

Ford: Moruya.

Forehead: Goolengdoogee.

Forest: Jinnetberrin; Wardulup; Wirrega.

Forest Oak: Buruda; Holpin.

Fork and **Forked:** Kalgoorlie; Koolanjin; Narra-; Narrabri.

Fresh Water: Gabeegong; Jennacubine; Waawaarawaa; Yampi; Yelleyellup.

Friends: Markaling.

Frilled Lizard: Ginairrunda; Kanni.

Frog: Carcoar; Junee; Kyarran.

green: Nudgee.

many: Bong Bong.

small: Nangkita.

Frost and **Frosty:** Barbigal; Murrarogan.

G

Galah Bird: Gillawarna; Gular; Gulargambone.

Game Animals:

no: Boonoo Boonoo.

plenty of: Jumbullah; Murrumbong.

Games: Dumbleyung.

Gap: Wilcan; Wilcannia.

Garden: Cabbaga.

Garments: Warrah.

Gather: Kunghah.

Gazing: Umbango.

Geese: Kiavolo.

Get Down: Bereowaltha.
Get On: Genanaguy.
Ghost: Muckiwinnormbin.
 place of: Kybybolite; Meley-
 maning; Yandembah.
 water hole: Ouyen.
Giddygiddy Bird: Cudgegong.
Girl: Lowanna; Mungon;
 Yeran.
 little: Gathong.
 pretty: Minil; Moogal.
Glade: Gooraman; Gooramma;
 Graman.
Glossy: Indiamba.
Glutton: Tuckurimbah.
Go, Going and **Gone:** Nardoowage; Woolrabunning.
 away: Bumbulla; Towang;
 Woolkabunning; Yallah.
 back: Mirregarng.
 round: Gooraway.
 where are you going?: Wahlooga; Wyengoo.
Goanna: Crudine; Dungate;
 Dungatewakaah; Geary-
 wah; Jerrawa; Narrandera;
 Unnaro; Yongurra.
 plenty of: Roba.
 walk about: Koolamur-
 tanaila.
God: Navimbarra.
Good: Budgeree; Marooan;
 Marook; Marumba; Mur-
 rumba; Murumba.
 luck: Eumminbung.
 path: Kulgun.
 people: Mushwandry.
 place: Quarbing.
 very: Budgerie; Cadgee.

 view: Tillabudgery; Wee-
 milah.
 water: Oulnina.
Good Day: Bathanny.
Good Morning: Kooraegulla.
Goodbye: Cuttebarley; Wabalingo.
Goodwill: Talofa.
Gooseberry: Brewarrina.
Gorge: Cubbletrenock; Gooro.
Grandfather: Cobargo.
Granite: Tibooburra; Wudina.
Grass and **Grassy:** Boorlahboorloo; Butho; Gilba;
 Gilgai; Kilto; Wudjong-
 moorjung.
 burnt: Gidgaween; Kulla-
 teenee.
 country: Midgee; Tyagarah.
 long: Bumboah; Chepperrup;
 Ejuncum; Groongal; Ura-
 wilkie; Warrambool; Warrnambool.
 plenty of: Chepearrup;
 Goanah; Jabbarup.
 wiry: Tamban.
 young: Budjewy.
Grasshopper: Bindowan;
 Neenan.
 land of: Temagong.
 plenty of: Oolambulla.
Grass Tree: Cooranggoorah;
 Dakkabin; Taplan; Tim-
 barra.
 place of: Keelkeelba. \
 ridge: Boogoolum.
Gravel: Cowrang; Wallinuninnie.
Great: Burra.

Great Spirit: Baiami; Byamee; Kiama.

Greedy: Punkally; Tomki.

Green: Cubbacubbah; Patawilya; Willamulka.

Greeting: Kooraegulla.

Grey: Pachomai.

Grind: Wagga Wagga.

Ground: Arrolla.
  beautiful: Terrabulla.
  cleared: Carara; Uyarrin; Wirega.
  dry: Benhennie; Durran Durran; Uloom.
  hard: Bumgum; Bungumme; Wollongong; Wollun.
  hole in the: Wollongbar.
  red: Melnunni; Wilgerup.
  sounding: Tumbarumba.
  white: Boonoona.

Grub: Barra; Coomorooguree; Jerbam.

Gully:
  boggy: Mitdapilly.
  deep: Bundanoon.
  flying squirrel: Jebropilly.
  of leeches: Indooroopilly.
  sandy: Yeerongpilly.
  with flat rock: Mymuggine.
  with stream: Bingeering; Dugalup; Nabelmup; Wallarobba.
  with stumps; Curnoomgully.

Gum: Dundilkar.
  place of: Mancarbine.
  plenty of: Jenymungup; Junynnmgup.

Gum Tree: Kalangadoo; Krambakh; Mangiri; Me-

prupiping; Mungarra; Warracknabeal; Wirrabara; Wirraminna; Wirreanda; Yaruppe; Yerrinan.
  bark: Currunghi.
  blossom: Bungendorf.
  flat: Wirramatya.
  grey: Duckan Duckan.
  leaves: Cumboogie.
  plenty of: Horrowill.
  red: Ceron; Karrawirraparri; Knooticup; Tarpeena; Yarra.
  white: Cussrunghi; Dungay; Geearangrib; Ullamulla; Wendo.

Gun: Onnua.

Gypsum: Tubbo.

H

Hail: Dandaloo; Dundullimal.

Hailstones: Garrapun.

Hair: Booningie; Budgerahgum; Gooringaragunambone; Puranga.

Hand: Biroo; Murrawan; Tidnacornarrinna.
  injured: Marrapigup; Murrabungalgie; Murracompagoorandannie; Murragoedgoen.

Handsome: Bullengen.

Happy Place: Minbalup; Quindalup.

Harbour: Ulladulla.

Hard-bottomed: Karratha.

Hat: Coondoondah.

Haunted: Epuldugger; Wurra-

wana; Yungaburra.
Haven: Bodalla; Eurobodalla.
Hawk: Polona; Royalberra.
Hazel Nut: Koriminnup.
Head: Cobbadamana; Cob-
bora; Pullabooka; Taja;
Wanbobra; Warawollung.
band: Cobranaraguy.
covering: Dubbo.
koala: Yarrahapinni.
water in the: Kulpara.
Headland: Caloundra; Now-
norrup; Yamba.
Heart: Codobine; Toogoolawa;
Tugulawa; Wurrole.
Heat: Coraki.
Heel: Dunnangmumma.
Hen: Howregan.
Hermit: Mundamutti.
Heron: Poonboon; Traralgon.
Hibiscus: Talwurrapin.
Hiding Place: Yarra.
High: Bowral; Chinogan; Dan-
denong; Yareing.
land: Attunga; Binalong;
Coolongolook; Cooloon-
gatta; Croajingalong;
Gkoonwarra; Illawarra;
Turramurra.
Hill: Booyooarto; Borandijup;
Bourbong; Bundaleer; But-
taba; Darling; Gobleback-
inglup; Nardie; -o; Pin-
dari; Roolcarirultaduan-
naaram; Wangianna; Will-
yama; Yarrimup; Yunger-
up.
bare: Dungog; Earindi; Jindalee; Mardarweiry; Mor-

gyup; Nariah; Wallend-
been.
camp in the: Goorack
Goorack.
devils': Gailagup.
distant: Burri Burri.
end of the: Coreen.
flat-topped: Bibbakine.
four: Bulla Bulla.
green: Nioka.
large: Boodgerakarta; Bungendorf; Bywong; Coolan-
gatta; Deningup; Goorad-
jin; Mundanup; Uralla;
Wongyarra.
many: Callemondah; Jurin-
pudding; Kiaka; Pontapin.
red: Cudgegong; Willicking.
round: Gooraanghee; Noue-
boondie; Wemgowaa;
Yerdine.
side: Bimberdong; Liete-
linna; Nimoola.
small: Bangalow; Cartmeticup; Jinnetberrin; Mul-
lumbimby.
steep: Burraburoo.
stony: Conmurra.
two: Anakie; Bullatop;
Ulooloo.
Holding: Nubhoygum.
Hole: Gilgai; Innamineka;
Tarwonga; Tocumwal.
digging: Carripan.
in ground: Cooberpedy;
Warrangunnia; Wollong-
bar.
in hill: Benomera.
in rock: Doradeen; Titwinda.

in tree: Beerubri; Boningwee.

kangaroos scratching: Yongermoranelyeirup; Yoongarilup.

rats': Ingra; Umberumberka.

runaway: Kybybolite.

thunder: Marlomerrikan.

wombat: Womboyne.

Hollow: Berrico; Thirroul; Uralba.

rock: Gibber.

tree: Cudgelo; Dural; Ngeatalling.

Home: Canowindra; Goudjoulgang.

between the hills: Uralba.

my: Tabulum; Yoorooga.

of the lost lovers: Wandandian.

our: Wahroonga.

Honey: Cootha; Gnaroo; Koongool; Mannaw; Marbolup; Narromine; Warral; Willoring.

comb: Doogumburrum.

place of: Narrogal; Quangulmerang; Warialda.

Honeysucker Bird: Carabobala; Dougalook; Talarook.

Honeysuckle: Buderim; Coonawarra; Kadlunga; Marrilman.

Hops: Condobolin; Gilla; Watcham.

Hornet: Warroo; Yahwang.

Horse: Euraman; Gunderman; Wayandah; Yarramalong; Yarraman.

Hot: Grong Grong; Wallon;

Weegoolgurra; Wilga.

House: Gundimaian; Gunyah; Lietelinna; Mugra; Takumuna.

of white man: Gillamagong.

Hullo: Jerendine.

Hunger and **Hungry:** Cubery; Galga; Zach.

Hunter: Mindaribba.

Hunting: Burragorang; Cubbine; Quamara; Tintinara.

camp: Turramboyne.

ground: Appilayarowie; Burrandong; Burrangong; Coombimbah; Googee; Kurinai; Towri; Wagininup.

Hurry: Beerriwera; Berrabri; Berriwere; Burri; Murray; Thurrungo.

Hut: Myambat.

bark: Gundi.

crows': Wahgunyah.

many: Miamia.

one: Mulgunnia.

stone: Gibberagunyah.

stranger's: Borrika.

I

I Don't Know: Wonawotha.

Ibis: Balbirooroo; Tambaroora.

Ice: Barcoo; Budla; Parattah.

Initiation Ceremonies: Boorebuck; Borambola; Kiparra; Kubura; Weddin.

Initiation Ground: Boorpah; Borambil; Bourbah; Goonambong; Murrumburrah;

Nocuting; Ourimbah; Purpur; Tabrabucca; Yerin.

Injured: Dulcoon.

Inlet: Belongil.

Inquisitive: Coonabarabran.

Insects: Cobbenbil.

Ironbark Tree: Chungandoonmoneybiggera; Mookerawa; Tugrabakh.

Ironstone Ridge: Starra.

Ironwood Tree: Booyong.

Island: Baarrook; Bulba; Coyinguine; Quaringa; Warawitcha; Wauraltee.

Itch: Biningyarrah.

J

Jammed between Trees: Curban.

Jarrah Tree: Jeeljarrup.

Jay: Killanoola.

Jolly: Kindilan.

Joyful: Euroa.

Jumping: Bocobble; Daroobalgie; Gnurrlarkendockenerup; Kapunda.

Junction: Coolah.

K

Kangaroo: Bellata; Callanna; Coora; Goola; Maraju; Mashbalgadjerry; Moonavinbinbie; Taldra; Wamboingoolian; Wamboyne; Waranalin; Wombiana; Youcoora.

black: Nantabibbie; Nantawarra; Norogo.

brown: Wallaroo; Womboyne.

dancing: Legerup; Yongerlocelkucup.

feeding: Balargorang; Wombinebong.

female: Comboyne.

flat: Gugetup.

hunting ground: Appilayarowie; Kangaloola.

large: Bundarra; Mirribandini; Wonogarup.

leg, bone in: Pulbging.

mountain: Windjo.

place of: Kangowirranilla; Wambangalong.

plenty of: Merringurra; Quirinerup.

pouch: Dumbermanning.

red: Bygalorie.

scratching holes: Yongermoranelyeirup; Yoongarilup.

sleeping: Wirrasupenee; Yelgecup; Yeulup.

tail: Grooman.

teeth: Nampup.

young: Barrenjoey; Woolloomooloo.

Kangaroo Rat: Curtiupah; Wyalga.

Karri Tree: Wardulup.

Kept: Neergoolabulgra.

Kicked: Bobledigbie; Wilganbala.

Killed: Boomgarla; Goullan; Noona; Yerinandah.

Kingfisher: Berrimbillah.

large: Cookadinya; Currumburra; Kargon.

Kite Hawk: Boorah.

Knife: Duggie; Kiandra; Kungaree.

Kowhai Tree: Te Kowai.

Kurrajong Tree: Kurrajong.

L

Lagoon: Bellbourie; Beregegama; Collie-; Miena; Wood-
enbong; Yalleroi.
crocodile in: Gongora.
deep: Woy Woy.
large: Belubula; Bunna Bunna; Goodooga; Goonal;
Keera; Menangle; Mung-
yer.
lilies in: Lurr.
long: Collymongle.
with wildfowl: Woorroo-
woolgan.

Lake: Burrumbeit; Cargelligo;
Comba; Iloura; Kamo;
Mooball; Quaberup.
crater: Barrine.
dry: Murninni.
large: Bandup; Cooma.
near: Yukieyackine.
small: Buckalow.
snakes near: Nunagin.
two: Merimbula.
white: Mookimba.

Lame: Dapto; Uga.

Lancewood Tree: Eyerah;
Moolcha.

Land: Coombabah; Dowcan.
red clay: Willakulin.

where sun rises: Wareelahcohgarra.
where sun sets: Kanandah.
white, on coast: Belardoo.

Land Crab: Booroogum.

Large: Booral; Marawell.

Last Man: Minane.

Last of Water: Toolaburroo.

Laughing: Murrungundie;
Withamango; Yamble.

Laughing Jackass: Carcoar;
Coogongoora; Goodawada;
Karkuburra; Kookabookra;
Quoak.

Lava: Leura.

Lawyer Vine: Boondarn; Nubhoygum.

Lazy: Milamunda.

Leaning to West: Marracoonda.

Leatherhead: Gulgorah.

Leaves: Comboogie; Urangbil.

Leaving: Mogurah.

Leeches: Biraganbil; Birragan-
bill; Indooroopilly; Toorong.

Left-handed: Merah; Woram.

Leg: Goonderin; Pulbging;
Warrapanillamullolacoo-
palline.

Lice: Tooloom.

Licking: Werthelwa.

Lies: Mudgeerabah.

Light: Kianga; Nargong.

Lightning: Malagara.
place of: Mickibri.
trees struck by: Bahwindundah; Bingarrah; Corobi-
milla; Marogi; Micabil;
Micke; Micketeeboomul-
geiai.

Lillypilly Tree: Oowan.
Lily: Ballowrie; Brinawa; Buribuca.
  large: Gymea; Minmi.
  plenty of: Wercan.
Limb: Bunglegumbie.
Liquid: Cowiaurita.
Limestone: Guniwaraldi.
Lime Tree: Tamborine; Tarampa; Taroom.
Liquor: Cooloni.
Listening: Twonkwillingup.
Little: Merang; Winnunga.
Liver: Thabbat.
Lizard: Mungiebundie; Nelaungaloo.
  place of: Murtoa; Narrandera; Umungah.
  plain: Kadina.
  sleeping: Banyam; Bowyum; Bunnerong; Caltowie; Larrawallup; Pwooyam.
  small: Kadungle; Nana.
Lobster: Perinyelup.
Locusts: Bran Bran.
Log:
  burnt: Marradong; Ulandi.
  chips cut from: Kindee.
  high up: Moobalinbah.
  large: Yulgilbar.
  mopoke in: Tuorodon.
  place of: Dilladerry; Gineroi.
Long: Goora.
Long Way: Yurgo.
Look Out!: Werai; Wollomai.
Look-out: Bibbenluke; Coolangatta; Cooloongatta; Dundeppa; Woollahra.
Lost: Nanima.

  feathers: Weighknarlbup.
  lovers: Wandandian.
Love: Nardeeneen; Weja.
Lovely: Amaroo.
Low: Chinogan; Cootamundra.
Lucky: Coolbaroomookoo; Coolburoomookoo.
Lying: Tamalee.
  emu: Ooringuldain.
  kangaroo: Yelgecup; Yeulup.
  vine: Pini.
Lyre Bird: Caboon; Calboonya; Cullenbullen.

M

Madman: Wanga.
Maggots: Bugabada.
Magic: Narooma.
Magpie: Barow; Coolbart; Goonoonggeereby; Mittegong; Noorengong; Turrawan; Wantigong; Whippengong.
Magpie Lark: Broolgang; Clergin.
Mahogany Tree: Gunderlong.
Mallee Bird: Toora.
  nest of: Brymedura.
Man: Amah; Burra; Codobine; Garoolgan; Krowathunkoolung; Kurri Kurri; Marrapigup; Mirragurra; Tallebudgera; Wambidgee; Wybalena.
  blind: Goonoo.
  burnt: Cockelup.
  dead: Crumbana; Kumal; Moochingoo.

last: Minane.
left-handed: Woram.
old: Jerrabung; Kincumber; Moobeencultak; Pinnaroo; Romerah.
quarrelling: Wallerawa.
small: Murragonga.
tall: Gooradool.
throwing club: Boomooderie.
wild: Warrangle.
with bad leg: Goonderin.
with crooked knees: Mebboonignarlinup.
with sore eyes: Gundurimbah.
young: Koloona; Kubura; Murragang; Nubingerie; Tallimba; Twanginna; Yaraka.
Mangrove Tree: Berree; Kangiangi; Pitonga.
Manna: Coonatta; Cumbooglecumbong.
Many: Winninnie.
Marriage: Canindboary; Japergiling; Laragon.
Marshmallow: Tickera.
Meat: Walgeemarrbimcaring; Winangubba.
Medicine: Gerongar; Koona; Penterong.
Medicine Man: Nulungery.
Meeting of the Waters: Bombala; Bulahdilah; Carwoola; Coomealla; Cullenbone; Cullengoral; Echuca; Mareeba; Nimmitabel; Ninacoogerup; Tuckurimbah; Unanderra; Walgett; Wangaratta;

Wollombi; Wondecla.
Meeting Place: Burragah; Canberra; Coerabko; Gol Gol; Guntawang;Mannagining; Murrabrine; Rumbriah; Winninnie.
by the water: Ooldea.
chief: Katanning.
I met him there: Oumbigalneeong.
to count fingers: Merrgining.
Melon: Toowoomba.
Messenger: Namalata.
Meteor: Girilambone.
Middle: Gingham.
Mignonette: Goonong.
Milk: Mulkblourway; Nammoona.
Mine: Almaden; Pathur.
Miserable: Yueagie.
Mistletoe: Bellarinya; Topiely; Wilbriggie.
Mocking Bird: Yilvung.
Monster: Burrygup; Cooraburrama; Euraman; Wollongong.
Moon: Alkina; Dilgon; Getten; Jannali; Keeden; Keerang.
camped: Keewong.
eclipse of: Niangala.
full: Maccalla.
mad: Munmurra.
new: Pallano.
rising: Meekinhindunpup; Mukintundunrup.
Moonshine: Gillebri.
Mopoke: Noona; Tuorodon.
cave of: Wirmalngrang.
Moreton Bay Ash Tree: Cooran.

Mosquitoes: Boin Boin; Debing; Moondarrewa.
plenty of: Boui Boui; Cooplacurripa; Curragundi.
Moss: Gin Gin; Wondup.
Moth: Bogonk.
Mother: Adjee; Cartee; Nahvoung; Wyanga.
river: Onkaparinga.
Mountain: Babinda; Binya; Boorang; Bulga Bulga; Deerangoomar;Kongoola; Moonyugin; Moorak; Murrurundi; -o; Omeo.
barren: Gingilin.
blowing up: Coraki.
close by: Eabrai.
dead tree on: Quirindi.
flat-topped: Yeraberi.
isolated: Jillamatong; Jillamunna.
large: Arrabri; Bulga; Cundumbul; Dougan; Gimboolah; Keira; Kelpum; Kittani;Milliburingyango; Rumbriah; Wollumbin.
of the mists: Eungella.
round: Yuraraba.
rugged-topped: Burrinjuck; Cumboyne.
side: Boolooinahl.
small: Mittagong; Warrumbungle.
steep: Jingerah.
watcher on: Meebalbogan.
Mountain Devil: Mullawerring.
Mourning, Place of: Nungattah.
Mouth: Nundah.
Much: Boolgun.

Mud and **Muddy:** Barwon; Booleroo; Meningle; Moondoo; Mularabone; Mungery; Tobbery.
creek: Tarparrie.
flat: Woolowa.
I got in the: Morundah.
red: Renmark.
Mulberry Tree: Nunda.
Mulga Tree: Mulgawarrina.
flower: Oodnadatta.
Mullet: Coobyaangar.
Mushroom: Murgon.
Music: Weeamara.
Mussel: Caling; Kianee; Nyngan; Queeryourga; Torcomoora.
ground: Dowgimbee.
plenty of: Pitchicanana.
shell: Culing.
Mutton Birds: Nirrittiba.
Myrtle: Lillipilli.

N

Names: Mannagining.
Narrow Place: Bullon; Puntei.
Native Companion: Bralgon; Brigalow; Carathool; Cohuna; Cundumully; Goondorrabrolga; Kunlara; Kyogle; Taralga; Traralgon.
place of: Illalong; Wandilo.
Neck: Bimpi; Coorong.
Needle Tree: Carvie.
Needlewood Tree: Walabah.
Nephew: Nugoon.
Nest: Tillararra.

ants': Keirbarban; Purribangla; Wongybill.
bees': Mahyl; Medulegah;
Warroul.
crows': Cockamongar.
eagles': Boundahalcarra;
Tobagangang.
plovers': Buldthery.
wasps': Cobbi; Meprupiping.
water fowls': Morangarel.
Net: Cussigungaringhi.
Nettle: Mullock; Wagonga.
New: Taleeban.
place: Yeltukka.
Night: Bullawie; Cabbagee;
Muronbong; Oomcurry.
Night Owl: Book Book; Killie;
Kinka; Wangi Wangi.
No: Bellambi; Wonghi.
-good: Bellbudgerie.
-good fellow: Wodrabiggunni; Woodrabeeka; Wood-
ralliggunnie.
-good place: Muteroo.
Noise: Moombahlene.
North: Cogin; Kononda.
wind: Canomie; Tinbin.
Nose: Moora.
bleeding: Merrygoen.
Nulla Nulla: Mourrindoc; Tab-
ragalba.
Nut: Wodonga.

O

Oak Tree:
forest: Belar.
place of: Belaradah; Booroodabin; Browie.

plenty of: Ollpin.
red: Anurie.
small: Mercadool.
Octopus: Minil.
One: Cooma.
One-eyed: Milbong; Wogle.
Onion Brother: Nulcrawon-
tharena.
Orange Tree: Gibinbell; Mogil
Mogil; Mokeley.
Ornaments: Bengalla.
Outlaw: Yabbra.
Over There: Carra Carra;
Goondi.
Owl: Bookoola.
Oysters: Ballina; Kinninggere;
Koppio; Moneal Moneal.
place of: Munkel Munkel;
Piththungah.

P

Paddocks: Malleea; Nermone.
Paddymelon: Beom.
Painting: Mlonerabe.
Palm Tree: Bangalow; Culkinewarinebinelup.
small: Numminbah.
swamp: Gorrijup.
zania: Narooma.
Pandanus Tree: Tallah.
root of: Jumpinpin.
Paperbark Tree: Milina; Yumbuck.
Parrot: Beerburrum; Condercutting; Corella; Eurie
Eurie; Warooka; Wira-
gulla.
bayonet bill: Dowarran.

Blue Mountain: Chumparia;
Jembyrinjah.
far away: Parragundie.
green: Berriwilliman.
king: Beeburing.
lory: Bolan Bolan.
place of: Billinooba; Parraweena; Wilgarning.
plenty of: Billinudjel; Cuttyguttygang.
rosella: Colac; Darile;
Gootering; Milbrulong.
twenty-eight: Damolock.
Parry: Gummin Gummin.
Passage: Curbanmah.
Path: Kulgun; Nangwarry;
Yandina.
Peaceful: Anembo.
Peaches: Murdong.
Peak: Nimbin.
Pebbles: Ellengerah.
Peeweet: Pimpama.
Pelican: Balonne; Tellegaree.
corroboree ground: Choon-
gurra.
feather of: Minarcobrinni.
plenty of: Cunygera; Dagamgurra.
plucked: Minacrobrinni.
water hole: Pulchra.
Peninsula: Kuttai.
People:
bad: Musero.
good: Mushwandry.
in forest: Wirrega.
Peppermint Tree: Gibberagee.
Perch, Fish: Mugerne.
place of: Orara.
Pheasant: Joalah.

Pigeon: Meriwolt; Wonga.
bronze-wing: Tahmoor;
Wabba.
call of: Quabothoo.
mating place: Tarrawonga.
place of: Yarrawonga.
topknot: Quabathoo.
Pigface: Bubbracowie.
Pigment: Kopurraba; Mirrool;
Purribangla; Weedlealby.
Pine Tree: Bugwanada;
Corowa; Currumbin;
Nomenade.
bunyabunya: Bonyi.
hole in: Boningwee.
place of: Bingamon; Cara-
watha; Goorabil; Goorari;
Koorawatha; Nallabooma.
plain: Cutchup.
plenty of: Pimbaacla.
ridge: Wiangarie.
scrub: Uambi.
Pipeclay: Cringila; Dullungil;
Mogo.
place of: Milingandi; Pitoba.
plenty of: Gumma Gumma.
Pipis: Jelleejuddo.
Pitchery: Pichirichi.
Place:
bare: Narriah.
beautiful: Coorumbene;
Illowra; Kiah.
cold: Iggin; Mulgarnup.
dirty: Goonambil.
good: Bredlaboura; Cudgee;
Jarramarumba; Merriwa;
Quarbing.
happy: Minbalup; Quinda-
lup.

haunted: Epuldugger; Yungaburra.
lovely: Amaroo.
narrow: Puntei.
new: Yeltukka.
no-good: Muteroo.
nondescript: Bengeaccah.
of plenty: Warrnambool.
of rest: Warrina.
open: Curracobark.
peaceful: Anembo.
pleasant: Elouera; Illawarra.
sheltered: Woolway.
sleepy: Numby Numby; Yengarie.
slippery: Tallawarra.
stopping: Warbroon.
surrounded by water: Gnahrool.
unhealthy: Dulcoonghi.
warm: Warrambucca.
waterless: Cowardine.

Plain: Corama; -long; Monaro; Patchieroombadillie; Perponda; Walloway; Yarraman; Yongerlocelkucup.
bushy: Boorthanna.
grassy: Midgee.
hill on: Wangianna.
long: Graman.
large: Boylegerup; Mirragurra; Quelquang; Tuggernong.
open: Dungarubba.
river on: Adelong; Bogobogalong; Nundahurrah.
rocky: Cutchup.
saltbush: Thulengar.

swampy: Galong; Geelong; Oolong.
waterless: Youring.
Planted: Goonoo.
Plants: Cundle; Deerangoomar; Demondril; Kuranda; Malla; Parakylia; Quinyum Quinyum; Teralba; Tharnkurruckkulk; Tregeagle.
Platypus: Noyumboon; Tungbung.
Playground: Murragang; Purryburry.
Playing: Weeraman; Yamble.
Plenty: Bullion; Coolabulling; Koora; Melinga; Thallmoy.
place of: Illowra; Warrnambool.
Plover: Balderodgery.
spurwing: Ditta Ditta; Jerry Jerry.
Plucking Feathers: Minarcobrinni.
Plum Tree: Karuah.
Point of Land: Koolywurtie; Korogoro; Mungerahbah; Tierabeenba.
Pointing: Toobeah.
Poison: Cobakh; Gillimanning.
Policeman: Cubtahpooliman; Tarboonpooliman.
Polygonum Bush: Willochra.
Pomegranate: Mogil.
Pool: Billabong; Bollup; Camphallup; Gigidin; Illabo; Jennacubine; Mallannyingah; Mollup; Moodyarrup;

Nardie; Tarragunda; Yelle-belling.

Poor: Bulkeewhirlbarr; Yueagie.

Porcupine: Caggaramabill; Kogoor; Muggi; Quandialla; Thargomindah; Tinnenburra.

place of: Gooninbah.

Porpoise: Gooulloah; Kooelung; Woy Woy.

Possum: Coomel; Guean; Ngeatalling; Tonggril; Willi Willi.

breeding place: Ulamambri.

catching: Willeyganalgee.

large: Willieploma.

place of: Guroura; Kynnumboon; Marree.

plenty of: Bungawitta; Coomaling; Gorrah; Murwillumbah.

ring-tail: Moira.

skin: Beltana; Dubbo.

small: Coonerang.

standing up: Williewarrina.

talking: Coomalwangra.

Potato: Jubuck.

Powerful: Matong.

Pretence: Merrewa.

Pulled: Wonthaggi.

Q

Quail: Beereegan; Bulberry; Moombindoo.

plenty of: Quilbone.

sound of: Urana.

Quandong: Bertical; Kulwararabooka.

Quarrelling: Wallerawa.

Quarry: Namogit.

Quartz: Calbertine; Uralba; Yilgarn.

Quick: Yrangie.

go: Yalla; Yarraking.

sand: Garriguronga.

Quiet: Anembo; Benbullen; Bullen Bullen.

R

Rain: Amarina; Bunna; Ermara; Goondam; Mokodabit; Mulwala; Wallah; Warrah.

no: Nourani.

plenty of: Bunna Bunna; Uranquinty; Walla Walla.

signs of: Warringah.

Rainbow: Wiberigan.

angry: Teerawah.

Rapid: Dundundra.

Raspberries: Illpah; Mulgulgum.

Rats: Candiup; Ingra; Moobor; Umberumberka.

plenty of: Kareelpa; Minganup; Quinginup.

Ravine: Gullallie.

Red: Coochin Coochin.

earth: Cudgen; Guaballing.

ochre: Gooraanghi.

Reed: Camira; Dugandan; Gnullum; Numira; Tucki Tucki.

floating: Wangdagup.

jiggi: Jiggi; Jiggijah.
large: Demondrille.
place of: Jerilderie; Jilderie;
Obley; Oodthulby.
standing up: Dreelwarrina.
swamp: Collaroy; Coogoo-
rah; Wilgo.
Refreshments: Gurrai.
Rejoicing: Talofa; Yoogali.
Reply to Little Ant: Dunowie.
Resting: Allawah; Ningana;
Quamby; Walkininnup;
Warrawee; Weenga.
crows' resting place: Wahgunyah.
here I rest: Leumeah.
place: Ballarat; Kywung;
Tumut; Warrina; Wee-
gerak.
turtle: Yackendahwirin.
Returning: Culgoa; Kulgoa.
Ribs: Donarah.
bloody: Gilgoenbone.
Ridge: Banyo; Dunoon; Moomoom.
grass tree: Boogoolum.
ironstone: Starra.
pine tree: Gooray; Wian-
garie.
red: Daymar.
stony: Bunyacubbol.
Riflebird: Bung Bung.
Ripple: Ulah.
River: Boggabilla; Coblinine;
Karrawirraparri; Nundah;
Nundahurrah; Pokataroo;
Tarup; Waarrar; Wam-
bool; Warawitcha; Worije.
banks: Giree Giree; Goyda;

Gurregory; Gwydir; Para-
chilna.
bend: Miandetta; Tarcoola;
Thelim; Ulmarra.
big: Barwon; Bonnonee;
Yagobie.
dry: Kalpara; Wannering.
mouth: Coraki; Culkine-
borough; Gorung; Nam-
bucca.
overflowing: Guagong.
sister to: Yacka.
small: Terranora; Thomar.
stony: Belubula; Corowa.
winding: Manilla.
Road: Dumpaal; Kullaroo;
Tharnkurruckkulk.
three: Yethera.
Roasting: Dookenine.
Rock: Berieel; Bojalup; Cowra;
Doongorwah; Jarara;
Jooriland; Kingimbon;
Mulumba; Thurlgona;
Wallungbogal; Wirrarie;
Wollondilly; Wolwollin.
bare: Balagup; Batagup.
black: Darkin; Woronora.
flat: Corramulling; Marreyourga; Mymuggine.
for sharpening axes: Trungley; Youndoogeedan.
granite: Bungawarrah;
Tibooburra; Wudina.
hollow: Doradeen; Gibber;
Titwinda.
kangaroo stuck in: Mash-
balgadjerry.
large: Gooraway; Mor-
borup; Nimbin; Wagnup;

Wooloongarra; Wordong-
guttergin.

plenty of: Currambine; Gibberagong; Molong.

red: Belladoonia; Coochiemudlow; Nangar.

split: Junnearupy.

three: Booradabie.

white: Bibanup.

Rock Adder: Cool; Coolootai.

Root: Borambil; Einbunpin;
Gerongar; Jumpinpin;
Koona; Kopperamanna;
Menigup; Mulgranah; Pen-
terong; Quagerup; Uki;
Warren; Whian Whian;
Wyan; Yerrine.

Round: Goompie.

Runaway: Cumbingum; Kybybolite; Yabbra.

Running: Bangingoo; Bodalla;
Culgoa; Kulgoa; Yarraking.

Rushes: Berieel; Billanbri;
Capemount;Carbanup;Gun-
galla; Kalguddering; Ko-
garah; Kulguddering; Man-
jimup.

S

Sacred Stones: Noorooma;
Towradgi.

Sad: Manattarulla.

Saltbush: Thulengar.

Salt Water: Malabine; Shara.

creek: Booroogarrabowy-
raneyand; Kooparaback.

crossing place: Bingeraba.

pool: Jennacubine; Yelle-
belling.

Sand and **Sandy:**

bank: Cooma.

country: Balookyambut;
Booiyana; Murnal; Nar-
ringbunkarrinup; Naturi;
Quelquang.

drifting: Kurdnatta; Yooth.

gully: Yeerongpilly.

hills: Dyurarba; Gunna-
matta; Nallabooma; Nap-
pamerril; Patchieroomba-
dillie.

hills, big: Coolyaron; Pooncaira; Yathong.

hills, red: Cocamittanewannie.

hills, two: Miliabacoolah.

plenty of: Warragai.

point: Mungerahbah.

white: Cooluddagadden.

Sandmartin : Terrie Terrie.

Sandpiper: Billagoe.

Sap: Malaria.

Satin Bird: Giro.

Scars: Ganmain.

Scrub: Gayndah; Killawarra;
Murrabinna; Nurragi.

dense: Boondine; Durakai;
Karte; Moonta; Tillery.

oak: Pilliga.

pheasant: Thuntalbi.

plenty of: Kittani.

prickly: Oondooroo.

white: Geearangrib.

Scum: Kouming.

Sea: Ballah; Morandoo; Tingira.

at back of the world: Narka-
bunda.
camp by the: Elanora.
fresh water near: Gabagong.
hills near: Yungarup.
near the: Iluka.
Sea Snipe: Munnungngurraba.
Seaweed: Bombery; Wootheroo.
floating: Koongburry.
place of: Kairaraba.
rotten: Coogee.
Seeds: Coomooroo; Gulligal;
Kooloobong; Tarcutta.
plenty of: Koolatai; Mer-
rina.
Seeing: Na.
Settle Down: Quamby.
Sewing: Curbollie.
Shade and **Shady:** Balatquitting;
Broomoing; Marloognunah;
Mongoluring; Mooldup;
Mowla.
Shadows: Onkaparinga.
Shag: Baratta; Birriebongie;
Goondiwindi.
black: Kunjavurra; Tara-
goro.
nests of: Wangaratta; Yar-
rawonga.
Shallow: Quaama; Tindarra.
crossing: Tullalar.
Sham: Merrewa.
Shark: Tinonee.
bitten by: Tallebudgera.
place of: Nurrungbah; War-
richatta.
Sheep: Bullo; Kangarilla.
Shells and **Shellfish:** Cabramat-

ta; Gnarriatta; Marami;
Weelu; Yalata.
Creator of: Beeroogoon.
mussel: Culing.
place of: Maroubra; Ugerebar.
plenty of: Gongeway; Jer-
cruba.
small pink: Cronulla.
Shelter: Gunyah; Ollpin; Tantanoola; Woolway.
deserted: Bungunya.
good: Goline.
She-oak: Binnum; Karkoo;
Kooringa; Narrung; Witg-
weri.
Shield: Bugar; Bulgan; Numurkah; Towrang.
painting: Mlonerabe.
parrying: Gummin Gum-
min.
small: Hillamah.
Ship, Shape of: Burrahbaa.
Shoal Water: Tappin Tappin.
Shoulder: Canobolas.
Shouting: Kungala.
Shovel: Kiacatoo.
Shrub: Ewingar; Hookina;
Milai.
Sick and **Sickness:** Arengarie;
Bungara; Dulcoon; Min-
gay.
corner: Dulcoonghini.
people: Inglegar; Willama-
long.
recovering from: Yiddah.
Signs of Water: Yamagulli.
Similar: Wowine.
Sinew: Comarra; Gundagai.

Singing: Bobra; Mangoplah.
　creek: Eungai.
Sister: Carathee; Yabboine.
Sitting: Allawah; Gunggari;
　Wybalena; Yangalla.
Skin: Bokaring; Jindalee.
Sky: Darel; Harah; Kurnalpi;
　Tintinara.
Sleep and **Sleeping:** Kamarah;
　Langaur; Quamby; Wan-
　gurra; Wirrinya; Woo-
　nona.
　camp: Toowacka.
　can't: Mugimullen.
　eels: Jerrara; Parramatta.
　kangaroos: Wirrasupenee.
　lizards: Larrawallup;
　Pwooyam.
Sleepy Place: Numby; Numby
　Numby; Yengarie.
Slippery: Tallawarra.
Small: Nyrang; Midgee;
　Nerang; Winnunga.
Smell: Booka Booka; Moo-
　genallin.
　of turtle: Budgimby.
　you: Boothaguo.
Smoke: Dirkah; Gooung;
　Pothana; Togar.
　cloud: Booyoolie.
　place of: Boodup; Boyup;
　Cajildry; Kapunda; Win-
　gen.
　small: Earamboo.
Smooth: Indiamba.
Snail: Bangaum.
Snake: Pitonga; Tumbilmullah.
　bearded: Koorakooraby.
　bitten by: Turrongoouddi.

black: Moondah; Moto;
　Narara.
brown: Tooraweenah.
carpet: Caboolture; Cobbal;
　Merroing; Wogalup.
creeping: Duri; Nindooimba.
diamond: Mugga.
large: Merimbula.
plenty of: Bidaminock;
　Munagin; Nunagin; Wag-
　galing.
sandhill: Womiulie.
tiger: Honka.
whip: Earin; Yeraran;
　Yourol.
Snapper: Walloo; Wollomi;
　Woolami.
Snow: Brewitataandee; Kun-
　ama.
Soil: Dulgambone; Goom-
　baban; Naturi; Wallinunin-
　nie.
Song: Marinna.
　of running water: Yanco.
Sorcery: Milang.
Sore Eyes: Gundurimbah;
　Mildura; Milparinka.
Sounds:
　crows: Wagga Wagga.
　hollow: Tumbarumba.
　jumping in water: Bumbal-
　dry.
　pigeons: Quabothoo.
　quails: Urana.
　rippling water: Keelbubban.
　turkeys: Murrumurro.
　waves: Bondi.
South: Berrima; Moruya.
　wind: Booran; Kareelah.

Southern Cross: Goondooloo; Mirrabook.
Sparrow Hawk: Callan; Carrican; Gigil; Milgin Milgin.
Speaking: Junee; Minnunggorana.
Spear: Becchal; Bimblegumbie; Birool; Bungulla; Dooloo; Kechualing; Mairmudding; Millaguin; Murrawombie; Tuan; Whian Whian.
  barb: Darraring.
  broken: Geetchboordankendoo; Gutchboordankendockenarup; Toolabidjael; Windaaning.
  head: Calannie; Tarup.
  ironbark: Kanaipa.
  long: Tunabidgie.
  many: Thullutheroey.
  place for making: Thullugnethgie; Tullibigeal.
  reed: Jerula.
  short: Toolamanang.
  timber for making: Corowa; Demondril; Goodawadda; Keechipup.
  two: Bullamwall.
  white man: Ongunajha.
  woman's: Whyneema.
Speargrass: Kooyalee.
Spearwood: Coolingup.
Spider: Curragundi; Marrar; Teemenaar.
Spinifex: Gorimu.
Spirit: Bruthen Bruthen; Coomburra; Thaahmarlkeepenk; Wandoowandong.

Great: Biami; Byamee; Kiama.
  place haunted by: Bidaminock; Coonkie; Nargan; Yungaburra.
Spittle: Karaak.
Splinter: Turrabom.
Splintered: Dilga.
Split: Banda Banda; Junnearupy; Tullibigeal.
Spoiled Wood: Wandong; Waurdang.
Spring: Balatquitting; Beetaloo; Boonooloo; Bulganinup; Bungarra; Coorrabin; Coulta; Curra-; Ganibup; Kamber; Koorakooraby; Manoora; -ong; Tallong; Waggaling; Willyoogup; Yelleyellup; Yoganup.
  among rocks: Gobblin; Wordonguttergin.
  boiling: Nelshaby.
  dry: Killiting.
  good: Cundugyup; Woodenbalup.
  in forest: Gabelbuttering.
  in valley: Aroona.
  large: Kolyourgouring; Moree.
  many: Carranaggin.
  nest of: Tillararra.
  on mountain: Badine; Bathillboro; Corrobora.
  place of: Nangawooka.
  small: Nigigin; Tundigup.
  stinking: Goonaring.
  two: Edillilie; Welgalling.
Springing up: Kringen.

Squeaker Bird: Belbucanina; Gulark.
Squirrel: Corranewarran; Tibrogargan.
Stake: Durrumbi.
Standing: Booka.
  alone: Nimbuwah.
  man: Brewarrina.
  possum: Williewarrina.
  stone: Degilbo.
Star: Calca; Guoingon; Kalbar; Kootingal; Meee; Rajah; Tintinara.
  bright: Inderwong.
  place of many: Girilambone.
Stealing: Winangubba.
Steep: Beddi; Nimoola.
Stick: Boomi; Tulla.
  bent: Curringbung.
  blackboy: Marbolup; Narrabri.
  forked: Koolanjin.
  paddymelon: Babarra.
  pathway of: Cannawigra.
  woman's hunting: Wanerrah.
Stinging Fish: Gruegarnie.
Stinging Tree: Burrayangatti; Geerydjine; Gympie; Tyeebin.
Stingray: Kurrawah; Nyaparrlenye.
Stinking: Booka Booka.
  camp: Eurabuga.
  seaweed: Coogee.
  spring: Goonaring.
Stone: Burra; Garradarrow; Padulla; Tarro; Wallabadah;Wallundwong;Whriba.
  broken: Turrabirren.

green: Willamulka.
hill of: Gkoonwarra; Mardarweiry; Morgyup.
hut: Gibberagunyah.
large: Booyup; Caddajin; Curragurra; Goorawan; Nimbin; Rulwalla.
plenty of: Kindaitchin; Mogil Mogil.
quartz: Uralba.
red: Myoonmyooan.
rocking: Pirrama.
sacred: Narooma; Noorooma; Towradgi.
sharp: Kiandra.
small: Karrara; Wubbera; Yarraldool.
under water: Burrabira.
white: Guniwaraldi; Gunnedah; Gurin Gurin; Wallumburrawang.
yellow: Goonagoora; Konakonabe; Myoonmyooan.
Stony: Yallaroi.
  country: Booderoo; Budumba; Narraburra; Terramungamine.
  hill: Wallendbeen.
  place: Boonderoo; Murrabinna.
  river: Belubula.
Stopping: Bearing; Nardoowage; Quamby.
  place: Balyarta; Paruna; Warbroon; Weegerak.
Storm: Goondah; Goong; Kamarga.
Storm Bird: Woringerong.
Straight Line: Coraperena.

Stranger: Wynarka.
two: Yanbulla.
Stream: Para; Wallarobba; Winderlup; Yarrangobilly.
bed: Warrambool.
dingo crossing: Worragalla.
going up: Gundagai.
house by: Gundimaian.
in gully: Gabyellia; Nabelmup.
Stringybark Tree: Dorrigo; Goondi; Gundi; Gundy.
Strong: Korewal; Matong.
Struggling: Boorraiberrima.
Stump: Bukkulla; Koorarawlyee; Merungora.
many: Cookamobila; Curnoomgully.
Stupid: Wallanbillan.
Subterranean Water: Parrakie.
Sugar: Gurranong.
ant: Googean.
bag: Mahyl.
Sulky: Millgetta.
Summer: Booragul; Dyum; Lowalde; Thureel.
water all: Wardup.
Sun: Allunga; Euro-; Euroka; Momite; Ra; Walcha; Yelgun.
rise: Dhoonywulgunny; Thoar; Wareelahcohgarra.
set: Dhoonygooroonthie; Ill-illiwa; Kanandah; Wongayerio.
Surface: Awaba.
Swallow: Illabunda; Nanardine.

Swallowing: Urrabirra.
Swamp: Belaring; Boranup; Bungawalbin; Cooki; Coolingup; Curdalup; Darlingup; Doolanghooterghu; Dungarubba; Goongiwarri; Kalangadoo;Menangle;Mordinup; Nanegup;Penola;Toorak; Toowoomba; Walginup; Wandilo; Warrnambool.
bitter: Burraga.
black: Coolringdon.
large: Bong Bong; Booligal; Brimbago;Bujerjup;Mickalamp.
long: Goorabin; Goorah.
many: Bungancoor; Bungyancoor.
palm: Gorrijup.
place of: Allora.
reedy: Coogoorah.
salty: Koolbung.
small: Mia.
white: Currambul.
Swampy Country: Boona; Galong; Geelong; Illalong; Mangurup; Mooroduc; Oolong; Tookayerta; Wagininup.
Swamp Gum Tree: Pata.
Swamp Mahogany: Gunning.
Swamp Oak Tree: Karakanba; Pilliga.
Swan: Ceolgerk; Dunedoo; Kinnibill; Rewring; Rungie.
alighting: Marleyquachyockup.

black: Bandyup; Kingurra; Maroochy.
call of: Knonghetup.
place of: Burrendah.

Swearing: Wodrabiggunni; Woodraliggunnie.

Sweet: Kadlunga; Reka.
food: Cumbooglecumbong.
water: Minlacowie; Tomago.

Sweetheart: Colliet; Warrin-giddy.

Swimming: Yarramar.
away: Baanbaa.
fish: Queerbri.

Swimming Place: Bukartilla; Coalbaggie; Kiemai.

Sword: Bangan.

T

Tadpole: Geerymbeerindal.

Tail:
dingo: Coombullnee.
kangaroo: Grooman.
shape of: Nendanup.

Take it: Muttama.

Talk and Talking: Myalla; Oah; Wangary.
possum: Coomalwangra.

Tall: Goora.
man: Gooradool.

Tallow Wood Tree: Wongah-gah.
crooked: Clybucca; Kalli-bucca.

Tarantula: Marrar.

Teacher: Minimbah.

Tea-tree: Moonoomgah; Rangal.

place of: Toorak; Yallatup.
red-flowering: Biwongkalla; Nambour.

Teeth: Wirrabilla; Wirrah; Yarraman.
knocking out: Bouradie; Yerin.
-like: Tierabeenba.
plenty of kangaroo: Nampup.

Temper, Bad: Coolah.

That Fellow: Gnijong.

Thicket: Keechipup.
blackboy: Ingenup; Yerda-nup.
wallaby: Goodalup.

Thigh: Darra; Moppin; Un-garie.
bone of kangaroo: Jule-mering.
broken: Terramungamine.

Thorn: Gibboke.

Throwing Stick: Wimmera; Womerah; Woomera.

Thunder: Gayndah; Maloo; Maralinga; Maroubra; Mitta Mitta; Murrobo; Tharah.
hole: Marlomerrikan.

Ticks: Cooloon; Tooloom.
kangaroo: Coolibullup.

Tide: Iarranguatta.

Timber: Goodawadda; Kalyra; Tomanbill.

Toad Fish: Croki.

Tobacco: Kuac.

Today: Yagoona.

Toes: Warrawarratinna.

Tomorrow: Neago.

Tongue of Land: Tallong.

Top, Put it on: Barathawomba.
Tortoise: Binkenbar.
Tossing up: Bodalla.
Track: Calyeeeruka; Chidna; Dumpaal;Jamberoo; Murrembidgee.
three: Kalgoorlie; Yethera.
Trading Place: Mandurah.
Tread: Cobbora.
Tree: Cobakh; Colane; Coonatta; Dunbible; Eumungerie; Magakine; Milai; Mungyer; Tulla; Wondergetup.
berry-bearing: Warrangong.
broken: Dilga.
burnt: Carbuckin; Moorombunnia.
cut down: Galantapa.
dead: Coobungo; Gineroi; Quirindi.
drooping: Goolamera.
evergreen: Wangi Wangi.
green: Willowie; Willunga; Wirrawilla; Yanagin.
hole in: Beerubri.
hollow: Cudgelo; Dural.
honey from: Willoring.
large: Battunga; Budgeribong; Quean; Tumbiumbi; Ulandi; Wandearah; Yarrunga.
of curiosity: Wacknarungyuka.
one: Eurunderee; Myallmundi;Roolcarirultaduannaaram.
plenty of: Banyula; Borallin; Cowgongi; Madabareenah; Quandline; Tallangatta; Yurrah.
root: Whian Whian; Wyan.
small: Ewingar; Illawambra; Tunnimgah.
struck by lightning: Bahwindundah; Bingarrah; Chungandoonmoneybiggera; Corobimilla; Marogi; Micabil; Micke; Micketeeboomulgeiai.
taking up: Pulletop.
two forked: Currabubula.
water from: Kalgoorliegynyah.
with lumps on trunk: Belingbak; Kiwarrick.
Troopers: Bulligema.
Tunnelling: Burgooney.
Turkey: Boongun; Boorowa; Bublara; Burrowa;Coraki; Cumble; Gheera; Julago; Keira; Kurrawonga; Kyogle; Numulgi; Tarraganda; Toongi; Wahgumpah.
call of: Murrumurro.
plenty of: Walloway.
Turpentine Tree: Pooraka; Yanderra.
Turtle: Boorinine; Cawana; Cootamundra; Currikee.
creek of: Purpur.
place of freshwater: Pinkenbah.
plenty of: Carbinup; Sparindeen.
resting on water: Yackendahwirin.
smell of: Budgimby.

Twisted: Narraburra.

Two: Bulla-; Nowra.

U

Ugly: Gooallie.

Uncle's Wife: Pamandi.

Understanding (I understand you): Biala; Yamadagool-burra.

Unobtainable: Bringelli.

V

Valley: Jindabyne; Megalong; Thirroul; Wangrah.
of plenty: Numeralla.
pleasant: Nutheram-natherann.

Vermin: Moonyugin.

Vexed: Coolah.

View, Good: Cooloongatta; Mourabimerri; Taronga; Til-labudgery; Weemilah.

Vine: Binbilla; Boondarn; Bun-dall; Kuorigoora;Nubhoy-gum; Pini; Walkeroon; Wooroongarry.
place of: Terragong.

W

Waddy: Choonnanging; Ko-tara.

Wait:
a while: Allambee; Gowa-yoo.
for me: Warathar.
here: Weddin.
here till I come: Kameruka.

Walk: Dowcan; Yandina.
crows: Thulley.
goanna: Koolamurranaila.

Walkabout: Cundiah; Dhoora Dhoora.

Wallaby: Burrill; Yuluma.
black mountain: Wallaroo.
old man: Wangun.
plenty of: Moonkoon.
red: Baradine.
rock: Wirreanda.
small: Patonga.
thicket: Goodalup.
young: Woonona.

Wanting:
don't want it: Waniguday.
what do you want?: Wid-giewas.

Warm Place: Warrambucca.

Washaway Water: Tarcowie.

Wasp: Temagog; Yahwulpa.
nest: Cobbi; Meprupiping.

Watcher: Meebalbogan.

Water: Chullundie; Comoo; Cullengoin; Ellingerah; Gab-; Gumbowie; Kal-goorliegoonyah; Kango-wirranilla; Kooringa; Magakine; Milparinka; Mudamuckla; Mulgowrie; Mundi; Nattai; Nyjong; Pinneena; Prahran; Why-alla; Willowie; Wirramin-na; Wollithiga; Yunderup.
bad: Babawalthi; Kaghil.
big: Bogandilla; Cowan; Murrembidgee.
brackish: Bookabie; Boomi.

broad: Kollimungool.
bubbling: Boilyup.
clear: Mercowie; Quean-
beyan; Wyuna; Yallakool.
close to surface: Gabyon.
cloudy: Kollien.
curling: Collendina.
deep: Binda; Kewol; Mur-
rowolga; Woy Woy; Yar-
ramundi.
drinking: Bulong; Coacatocalleen; Gnullum; Nijong.
falling: Katoomba.
fresh: Akma.
from a hill: Coolumbla.
good: Condowie; Goonoo
Goonoo; Oulnina.
holding: Combok.
in head: Kulpara.
jumping into: Daroobalgie.
jumping out: Kapunda.
last of: Toolaburroo.
long: Bundarryuron; Gooraman; Kondoparinga; Wal-
langarra.
meeting of: Barellan.
meeting place at: Ooldea.
muddy: Barwon; Mulara-
bone.
near: Talia; Toongabbie;
Wattamolla.
no: Cowardine; Tangorron.
overflowing: Wilcan.
permanent: Dungullin;
Mundi Mundi; Wardup.
plenty of: Aldinga; Bodalla;
Bong Bong; Boonooloo;
Coobowie; Cullenbullen;
Dingabledinga; Drucwal-
la; Munbilla; Tarrawatta;
Tilba Tilba; Wallerawang;
Wharthum; Yarram; Yer-
yeri.
rapid: Mowonbymoney;
Thuddungra; Yerroulbine.
rippling, sound of: Keel-
bubban.
running: Aroona; Beltana;
Buckajo; Calwalla; Jim-
micubine; Mordiyallock;
Mungalkolli; Nadjonbilla;
Tirranna; Wandinyallock;
Wirrabara; Wyong; Yarra;
Yass.
running into hole: Tarwonga.
running over rocks: Goondiwindi; Wolwillin.
running, song of: Yanco.
signs of: Yamagulli.
shallow: Madabareenah;
Quaama; Tindarra.
shoal: Tappin Tappin.
small: Bardinnerrang; Mitta
Mitta; Willandra.
stones in: Goorawan.
subterranean: Parrakie; Toowoomba.
sweet: Minlacowie; Tomago.
trickling: Broula; Wollondilly.
two: Pambula.
where is the: Coominyah.
wide: Yarcowie.
Waterfall: Dundundra; Durradulee; Galliebarinda; Jakabulga; Quirindi; Urrugal-
gee; Yarram.
double: Yatteyatah.

eel escaped over: Turrum-
talone.

large: Bareemal.

Water Fowl: Bookinoragh;
Millelung.

nest: Morangarel.

Water Hole: Algebuckina; Barringup; Ceduna; Collie;
Colliup; Comba; Comba-;
Coombak; Curragundi;
Gourwin; Jooriland; Kiki;
Kootapatamba; Mandur-
ama; Nappamerril; Nun-
jikompita; Pulchra; Tin-
nenburra; Warrapanilla-
mullolacoopallinie; Wirrabilla.

chain of: Boorabbin; Gun-
aga; Nundah.

crows': Warcowie.

deep: Cullingral; Curra-
mulka; Daping; Gulgong.

ghost: Ouyen.

good: Boonderabbi; Coon-
derabbri; Gaberline.

in river: Coompagimpa;
Mungindie.

in sandhills: Cartalacoolah;
Wilgoyne.

large: Boronga; Collie-;
Gundaroo; Naracoorte;
Onaunga; Tarana; Whar-
kuroogma; Wolumla.

long: Gilgandra; Gullin-
goorun; Moree; Walgett.

many: Illbonden.

of sleepy lizard: Caltowie.

old: Killerberrin.

on the plain: Cutana.

rock: Canowie; Wirrarie.

round: Booborowie.

shady: Mowla.

three large: Wallatappe.

with fish: Piatarria; Quipolly.

Water Lily: Koolilabah; Lurr;
Turilawa; Yelarbon.

place of: Araluen.

Water Nymph: Lalaguli.

Water Rat: Moonoo.

Watershed: Boorgidjeagoorah.

Water Snake: Coyelgee.

Water Wagtail: Ichemen; Yerringhe.

Water Weed: Delungra; Moorungum; Turella.

Wattle Bird: Dougalook;
Morambro; Talarook.

Wattle Tree: Brigalow; Goomagully; Murengeriga.

black: Calume; Mumbil.

flower: Barreenong.

green: Yullundry.

place of: Boigon; Mimosa.

silver: Ferritcartup.

Waves: Bondi; Pinduro.

We: Alleena.

Weapon: Oodlawirra.

Weather:

cold: Bookra; Kallaroo.

fine: Jeedbowlee.

Welcome: Orana.

Well: Pathur.

West: Marracoonda.

wind: Deleanberry; Jungay.

Wet Country: Nounmoning.

Whale: Yooyoongan.

What do you Want?: Minago.

What is the Matter?: Naodaup.

Where?: Minore.
Whirling (pool and wind): Paringa; Woogaroo; Woolloomooloo; Woolooncappemn; Wooloongabba.
Whiskers: Nungeroo; Yarryn.
White: Bootha; Targan.
White Man: Mickelloo; Oimah; Tarboonenltak; Yararley.
  camp: Apurlu; Mantung.
  hole in ground: Cooberpedy.
  house: Gillamagong.
  policeman: Tarboonpooliman.
  speared: Ongunajha.
  with gun: Onnua.
White Woman: Tarboonkinkill; Yararleymerrigi.
Why: Minore.
Wide: Munna.
  river: Pokataroo.
Wife, Divorced: Myponga.
Wild: Warragul.
  fowl: Kembla; Tanunda.
  man: Bardoc; Warrangle.
  tribe: Warrigal.
Will Go There: Jingubullaworrigee.
Willow: Mungee.
Willy Wagtail: Dirigeree; Teckerrygorry.
Wind: Burraganbar; Coorain; Marbilling; Tharah; Witgweri.
  east: Wincey.
  north: Tinbin.
  south: Booran; Kareelah.
  strong: Camooweal; Marebone; Walgooan; Yeraan.
  west: Deleanberry; Jungay.
Winding: Manilla.
Windy: Booligal; Gadara; Mathoura; Taloumbi.
Wing: Currimundri; Waikerie.
Winking: Malbeling.
Winter: Muggora.
  camp: Karoonda.
Woman: Jundah; Yunta.
  bartered: Hennendri.
  beautiful: Merinda.
  by fire: Eenaweena.
  childless: Coonalpyn.
  climbing: Bunagan.
  fight over: Lridalah.
  fishing ground: Booragree.
  fond of: Kihi.
  hunting stick: Wanerrah.
  killed: Goullan.
  little: Bungledool; Eenerweena.
  old: Ivanjah; Thargobang.
  ravaged: Tarrana.
  river: Onkaparinga.
  runaway: Bepera; Cumbingun.
  spears: Whyneema.
  stout: Gurri.
  sulky: Millgetta.
  terror for: Combo.
  with child: Tatham.
  young: Kwinana; Mermerrah.
Wombat: Coolong; Mowbardonemargodine; Tyagong; Wombat; Womboyne.
Wood: Nundah; Wee; Yugilbar.

dry: Yarardup.
scarcity of: Weetaliba.
spoiled: Wandong; Waurdang.
Wool: Boonthno.
Woomera: Merilup.
Worm: Tyabb.
Wounded: Ballina.
Wren: Dendendaloom.

Y

Yam: Coobah; Koona; Noogoon; Tambo.
place of: Dumbum.
plenty of: Millnegang; Sheringa; Yowangup.
Yellow Jacket Tree: Taengarrahwarrawarildi.
You and Me: Nowra.
You Stay Here: Kalyan.

APPENDIX B

PRESENT DAY NAMES

with Earlier Aboriginal Names

Note: Names marked with an asterisk appear in the main list with meanings.

A

Abbotsford: Bigi Bigi.
Aberdeen: *Moonbil.
Acacia Creek: *Geearangrib.
Adelaide: Tandarnya; Tandarynga.
Albert, Lake: Yarli.
Albury: Bungambrewather.
Alexandrina, Lake: Kayinga; Mungkuli; Parnka.
Alfred, Mount: Teenarybilla.
Alice Springs: Tjauritji.
Alum, Mount: Minni Minni.
Amity Point: Brempa; Pulan.
Amoefield: *Walkeroon.
Anderson, Mount: Burruelby-ruie; Culcullin.
Anderson's Sugarloaf: Burral-burrie.
Angle Pole: Carulinia.
Anlaby: Pudna.
Anna Creek: *Kalachalpa.
Appin Falls: Currang Currang.
Appletree Flat: *Junburra.
Arbuthnot: *Warrumbungle.
Arthurville: *Gundy.
Aurora Creek: Wedoch.
Avenue Range: *Kalyra.
Avon River: Gogulgar; Gogulger.

B

Babel Knob: Odloopan.
Bakewell, Mount: Balladon.
Bannister's River: Gyngoorda.
Barker, Mount: Wommamu-kurta.
Barrietown: *Namogit.
Barron Falls: Biboohra; Kamerunga.
Batten's Bight: *Kianee.
Beachport: *Wirmalngrang.
Beenleigh: *Wobbumarjoo.
Bellinger Heads: Gelingenmeda.
Bellinger Peak: Conburragetin.
Bellinger River: *Bundarryuron.
Bell's Mountain: Millboorum.
Belmont: Goorgyp.
Bengulla: Beamadilla.
Berry: Bingin.
Bessibelle: *Killumboolth.
Bexhill: *Bullawhay.
Big Hill: Gooreejubba.
Billo Mountain: Millborum.
Billy Blue's Point: Warringarea.
Blackball Range: *Bonyi.
Blackbull Creek: Jeremeta.
Black Head: *Gearywah.
Blackman's Creek: Beeahgudabar.
Black Wall Reach: Jenalup.
Blue Lake: Waaor.
Blue Mountain: Ooralwilly.
Blue Mountains: Moorda.
Blue Nob: *Boolooinahl.

Blue's Point: Warungarea.
Bluff Mountain: Keerawak.
Bonney, Lake: Bonneia.
Boundary Creek: Egolwah.
Bourke: Nulta Nulta; Wurta-murtah.
Bradley's Head: Burragi; Bur-ragy.
Branxholm: *Mullock.
Bremer, River: Meechi.
Bribie Island: *Bongaree.
Brisbane: *Meannjin; *Kareel-pa.
Broadwater: *Keirbarban.
Broken Hill: *Willyama.
Brown, Mount: Booyeeanup.
Brownhill Creek: Willa Willa, Willaparinga;
Brunswick River: Durangbil.
Bungwall Flat: Bungwah; Jular.
Burie Creek: *Gruegarnie.
Burleigh:
  Big Burleigh: Jabbribillum.
  Little Burleigh: Jellurgul.
Burnett River: Birrabarra; Bor-rall Borrall.
Busby's Flat: *Wudjongmoor-jung.
Butler's Hump: Beereegup.
Butterbone: *Buddabone.

C

Camaroon: Cooenwarda.
Camden: *Benhennie.
Camera: *Burraganbar.
Campbell, Lake: Pidleewirra.
Cangi: Nubarragurra.
Canning: Booragoon; Dyarl-garro.

Cape River: Malangupbilea; Malangupbilla.
Careening Cover Head: Weye Weye.
Carnac: Ngooloormayup.
Caroline Pool: Wimery
Carron River: Arduna; Bitina.
Carwell: Midawarrie.
Casterton: Gnooloom.
Castle Rock: Coorumgoora.
Cathcart: Togranong.
Cherry Gardens: Pennachow-inga.
Cherry Gardens: Penna-chowinga.
Chowder Bay: Koree.
Clare: Kyneetchya.
Clarence River: *Booroogar-rabowyraneyand.
Clarke Island (Port Jackson): Billingoololah.
Cleveland Point: Nandeebie.
Cliffdale Creek: *Catthalalla.
Clontarf: Burrabra.
Clyde River: Bindoo.
Cockatoo Island: *Biloela.
Coff's Harbour: Corambara.
Coleraine:*Thahtoochthashurl.
Collins Flat: Kayjamee.
Condah: Nillunggeahurl.
Cooldale:.*Yerringhe.
Copp Harbour: Corambara.
Copmanhurst: Budgemby.
Cordeaux, Mount: Niamboyoo.
Cork Creek: Billeden.
Corrimal: Korimul.
Crawford, Mount: Teetaka.
Crawley: Goodamboorup.
Creen Creek: Karabelma.

Crooked Creek: Cumbucco; Nindalyup.

Crystal Brook: *Mercowie.

Cullen Point: Tullanaringa.

Cumberland: Aralgata.

Cundletown: *Kundle Kundle.

Cunningham's Gap: Cappoong.

Currency Creek: Bungung.

Cutham: Kangetmuning.

D

Dalkeith: Narnalguarh.

Darling Harbour: Tumbulong.

Darling Point: Eurambie.

Darling River Mouth: Tiltebaaka.

Dartbrook: Goonawidgera.

Dartmor: *Koonging.

Dead Dog Beach: *Moyekaeeta.

Deep Creek Mine: Nunoomerel.

Deepwater: *Dulgambone.

Delamere: Bullaparinga.

Delegate: Dilliget.

Dengate: *Dungate.

Denial Bay: Nadia.

Derrain: Dulladerry.

Diamantina, Mount: Toomathoogamie.

Digby: *Poormungburrh.

Dignam's Creek: *Wulunthar.

Dogtrap Creek: Ooriwi.

Doran's Hill: Meoloobinby.

Dorrigo, Mount: Nara.

Double Swamp: *Dundilkar.

Dromedary, Mount: Cubago.

Drumberg: *Thaahmarlkeepenk.

Dundab, Point: Barada.

Dunmore: Moonookkeyurl.

Dunwich: *Goompie.

E

Eacham, Lake: Yeetcham.

Eatonsville: Margungerie.

Edinglassie: Malgoorieyn.

Eliza Bay: Godroo.

Eliza, Mount: Gargatup; Karrakatta.

Elizabeth Point: Jerrewon.

Ellen Brook: Gynning.

Emily Spring: Munyoo-oolana.

Emu Creek: Undookatilly.

Emu Park: Woolpal.

Encounter Bay: Wirramula.

Enoggera: Enoggera.

Ernest Junction: Coombabah.

Escape Cliffs: Paterpurra.

Esperance: *Gabakile.

Etchells: Moombee Moombee.

Eucla: Chiniala; Yirculyer.

Eyre, Lake: Katitanda.

F

Fairfield: *Washimberribin.

Farm Cover: Woccannagully.

Fernmount: Bungiegumba.

Fig Tree Point: Cooroowal.

Fine Flower Creek: *Mungungboora.

Finke River: *Lirambenda.

Finley: *Carawatha.

Fish River Caves: *Benomera.

Fort Denison: Mattewanye.

Fort Macquarie: Jubaghalee; Jubughalie.

Fowler's Bay: *Yalata.

Fremantle: Walyalup.

Frenchmans, The: Jilling.

Freshwater Bay: Berragh; Minderup.
Furracabad: *Earindi.

G

Gambier, Mount: Erengbalam.
Garden Island: *Dundappi; Meeandip.
Gascoyne River: Tooricah.
Gawler: Kaleeya.
Gawler River: Mooleyerkeperre.
Gerrard Hill: Tookerimbah.
Gilbert River: Kenadla; Nambucca; Yambuccoua.
Gilston: Booiee Booiee.
Gladstone: Booyoolie.
Glenelg: *Patawilya.
Glen Innes: *Kindaitchin.
Goat Island: Melmel; Mil Mil.
Gordonbrook: *Pulbgin.
Gorge: *Burraganee.
Goulburn: Burbong.
Gragin: *Gooradjin.
Gravatt, Mount: *Caggaramabill.
Great Island: *Melmel.
Green Island: Tangeera.
Greville, Mount: *Meebalbogan.
Guildford: Mandoon.
Gum Tree Hill: Chilgungiree.
Gwyder River (upper part): Meei.

H

Hahndorf: *Bukarilla.
Hallett: Willogoleeche.
Hall's Creek: Sungoloo.
Hamilton: *Wunnuckin.

Hanging Rock Creek: Donigum.
Happy Valley: Wara.
Harris, Mount: Bebruebebundah.
Hastings, Point: *Kudgeree.
Hawkesbury River: Deerabubbin; Dooraban.
Heathcote, Point: Gooleegatup.
Helena: Mandoon.
Henley Park: Wurerup.
Herbert, Mount: *Booyooarto.
Herdsman's Lake: Ngoorgenboro.
Hillston: *Melnunni.
Hindmarsh Island: Kumarangk.
Hindmarsh River: Mootaparinga; Yalladoola.
Hindmarsh Valley: *Nangawooka.
Holme's Sugar Loaf: Columbin.
Hope, Lake: Pandopennunle.
Horse Bend: *Kooroomie.
Horse-shoe Lagoon: *Beregegama.
Hotspur: Boonbith.
Hunter River: Myan.
Hunter's Hill: Moocooboola.
Hurtle Vale: Kowiemunilla.
Hutt River: Parriworta.
Hydes Creek: Woodgerin.

I

Inglewood: Parrieagna.
Inman River: Moogora; Moooola.
Inverell: *Giree Giree.
Ipswich: Tulmur.

J

Jacob's Creek: Cowieaurita.
Jerseyville: *Cussrunghi.
Jervis Bay: *Bouderee.
Jinglemoney: Gengoming.
Juan and **Julia Rocks:** Salaama-
billigen.

K

Kangaroo Island: Karta.
Keira, Mount: *Gheera.
Kelmscott: Goolamrup.
Kembla, Mount: *Jumbullah.
Kenny's Creek: *Coombullnee.
King Island: Yeeroobin.
King River: Kalgan.
King George's Sound: Monk-
beeluen.
Kirkley, Mount: Gillingaram-
billy.
Kirton Point: Punnu Mudla.
Klemzig: Warkowoldiwoldi.

L

Lachlan River: Calar; Calara;
Callara.
Lady Macquarie's Chair Point:
Wiong.
Landsborough: Waroojra.
Lane Cove River: Turrumburra.
Lang's Point: Kabungbarra;
Kobungbarra.
La Perouse: *Korewal.
Larbert: Kouraduckbidge.
Laura: *Wirramatya.
Lavender Bay: Quiberee.
Leg of Mutton Lake: Yattonloo.
Lennard's Brook: Boora.
Lett, River: Tarrapalet.

Liddleton: Mooraminbilly.
Light, River: Yarralinka.
Lindenman Island: *Yarkiamba.
Lionsville: *Budgerahgum.
Lipson's Cove: Budlu.
Lismore: *Tuckurimbah.
Lismore South: *Pwooyam.
Little Bay: *Burraga.
Little Waroona Creek: Keurin-
gawarno.
Lofty, Mount: Yureidla.
Long Bay: *Mugga.
Longnose Point: *Yerroulbine.
Long Reach: *Getten.
Lookout, Mount: *Mourabi-
merri.
Lookout Point: Terangeree.
Lousey Point: Murrabale.
Louth Island: Yourunu.
Lyndoch: Putpa; Putrayerta.
Lytton: Alongpin.

M

Macclesfield: *Kangowirra-
nilla.
McDonald, Mount: Arachutta;
Chamerlina.
MacDonnell Bay: Ngaranga.
MacIntyre River: Karaula.
McLaren Vale: Dooronga;
Myallinna.
Macleay Point: Rauuki; Yar-
randabbi.
Macquarie River: Wambool.
Magnetic Island: Daggoombah.
Maitland: *Madiwaitu.
Maitland:
East: Cooloogoolooheit.
West: Boyen.

Manly: Narlung.
Mann River: Ballygul.
Manning River: *Cubbletrenok.
Mannum: Manumph.
Maroon, Mount: Wahlmoorun.
Marowon: *Horrowill.
Mary River: Goodna; Monoboola; Mooraboocoola; Yaboon.
Mary Pool: Keloo.
Medlow Bath: *Megalong.
Melville Water: Dootanboro.
Merino: *Thinggurrhmin.
Merton: Buneewo.
Middle Harbour: Warringa.
Middle Head: Barrabrai; Cubba Cubba.
Mill Point: Garrenup.
Miller's Point: Wodgee.
Milson's Point: Kiarabilli; Kiarabelli; Kirribilli.
Milton: *Uruthuck.
Minnie Pool: Roilo.
Misery, Mount: *Manattarulla.
Modbury: Kirraungdinga.
Monger, Mount: Tullanmingi.
Monger's Lake: Galup.
Montague Island: *Burrahbaa.
Moona Falls: Wooraway.
Moona Plain Mountain: Maramoonbang.
Moona Plains: Winboine.
Moreton Island: Gnoorganpin; Moaraganpin.
Morgan: Coerabko.
Mosman: Goranbullagong.
Mrs Macquarie's Point: Yourong.
Mud Island: Bungumba.

Murat Bay: Ceduna.
Murray Bridge: Mobilong.
Murray Estuary: Gilba.
Murray River: Different parts of river: Etandua (mouth); Goolwarra; Ingalta; Moorundie; Parriangkaperre; Tongwillum; Yoorlooarra.
Murray River: Meelon; Meeton.
Murray River Head: *Indi.
Mussel Creek: Gyarran.
Muswellbrook: Bimboorien.
Myall Creek: *Turrabirrin.
Myrtle Creek: *Muckiwinnormbin.

N

Nailsworth: Narnu.
Nettle Creek: *Dumbum.
Neutral Bay: Wirrabirra.
New Farm: Pinkenbah.
New Norcia: Maura Maura.
Newcastle: *Mulubinba.
Newinga: Noona.
Newry Island: Barlalimba.
Newstead: Karakaranpinbilli.
Newton Boyd: Begann.
Newton's Point: Camberramoueie.
North Harbour: Kunna.
North Head: Boree; Bunnabee; Bunnabri.
North Koppel Island: *Canomie.
North Lismore: *Banyam.
North Shore: Walamutta.
Northon's Gap: Kooumba.
Nullabor Plain: *Bunda Bunda.
Nunda Creek: Rollamota.

O

Ohio: Arounun.
Old Woman's Island: *Mudjimba.
Overton: Gola.

P

Parkes: Kurrajong.
Peak Hill: *Bibboorah.
Peake Creek: Wirriecurrie.
Peel Island: Jeerkooroora.
Pelican, Point: Boorianup.
Penrith: Mulgoa.
Percyville: Stampa.
Perth: Boorlo; *Burrell.
Pickering: Buburra.
Piercefield: Coogoowil.
Pinchgut Island: Muttawunga.
Pine Creek: Dularangi.
Pines, The: Yackaralthena; Yackarnathelka.
Pipe Clay Creek: *Mogo.
Piper, Point: Bungarung; Walara; Willara; Willarra.
Port Adelaide: Yertaboldinga.
Port Arthur: Premaydena.
Port Augusta: *Kurdnatta.
Port Hacking: Goonamarra.
Port Lincoln: Kallinyalla.
Port Macquarie: Goorook.
Port Pirie: *Tarparrie.
Potts Point: Curragundi; Currajeen; Yarranabbe.
Preston, Point: Niergarup.
Pumpkin Swamp: *Currumbungee.
Purfleet: *Turrabumbene.
Pyrmont: *Pirrama.

Q

Queen's Own Town: Watulunga.
Queensport: Maurira.

R

Raleigh: Dundangin.
Ramco: Dogorampko.
Ramornie: *Duckan Duckan.
Rapid Bay: Patpungga.
Redcliffe Point: *Umpiebong.
Redland Bay: *Talwurrapin.
Reedbeds, The: Witoinigga.
Remarkable, Mount: Willowie; Wongyarra.
Rese Valley: *Nutheramnatherann.
Rivoli Bay:
  Northern portion: Wirmalngrang.
  Southern portion: Wilichum.
Robertson's Point: Walwarrajeung; Wulworrajeung.
Roby Creek: Jingoll.
Rocky Bay: Garungup.
Rocky Point: Burraway; *Doogumburrum.
Rocky River: Wongabirrie.
Roebourne: Eromuckato.
Rosataca (The name is a combination of Rosewater and Yataca).
Rosebank: *Boiboigar.
Rose Bay: *Goudjoulgang.
Rose Valley: *Nutheramnatherann.
Rosebrook: *Coolumbla.
Rossgold: Tallagamaroongee.
Rottnest Island: Wadjemup.

Rushcutters Bay: *Kogarah.
Russell Island: Kanaipa.

S

St Ann's Hill: Ngowerup.
St Helena Island: *Noogoon; *Nugoon.
St Hilliers: Weedurran.
St Vincent's Gulf: *Wongayerio.
Sandgate: Warra.
Sandilands: *Bungumme.
Scrubby Creek: Wgandi.
Shark Island: Boambilla; Boambillia.
Shark Point: Burroway.
Shoalhaven River: *Bangalee.
Siddons Bay: Kulli.
Signal Point: Tapella.
Sirius Cove: Gorambullagong.
Skellatar: Tamundi.
Slaughterhouse Bay: Tarra.
Smoky Cape: *Gooung.
Snapper Point: *Wollomi.
Snowy River: *Mowon Bymoney.
Solander, Cape: Givea.
Solferino: *Duelgum.
Solitary, Mount: *Manattarulla.
Sorell, Cape: Panatama.
South Arm: *Dourim.
South Head: Burrawurra; Cuttai; Givea.
South Koppel Island: Wapparaburra.
South Molle: *Whriba.
South Woodburn: Munnenmeregan; Munnenuregan.
Sow and Pigs: *Birrabirra; Burrabira.

Spicer's Gap: Barguggan.
Spit, The: Burrabra; Burrabri; Parrawi.
Spring Cove: Wrrungli.
Stevenson's Creek: Ooljeraginia.
Stonehenge: *Holpin.
Stradebrake: Terangery.
Streaky Bay: Cooeyanna.
Sturt River: *Warriparri.
Sugarloaf: Cullurraba.
Swamp Oak: Weabonga.
Swan Bay: Widgeewidgeepin.
Swan River: Derbalyaragan; Derbalyaragon; Warndoolier.
Sydney: Warrane.
Sydney Botanical Gardens: Youlough.
 Clifton Gardens: Koree.
Sydney Cove: Warane.
Sydney, North: Walumetta.

T

Tailem Bend: *Thelim.
Tamar: Penrabbel.
Tatham: *Chargem.
Tenterfield: *Moombahlene.
Terrible Vale: Turrubul.
Teven: *Tyeebin.
Tom Ugly's Point: *Wogle.
Torrens, River: *Karra Wirra Parri.
 Other names for parts: Yertala (in flood); Korra Weera; Witoing.
Trawley: Goodabillow.
Tucker's Island: Menngarin.
Tunstall Gap: Cobaiwe.

V

Valley Lake: Kettla Malpe.
Vaucluse: *Kooelung.
Vaucluse Point: Moring.
Violet Lake: *Wiluna.

W

Wallis's Plain: *Boun.
Walter, Point: Dyoondalup.
Waroona Creek: Nagago.
Warwick: Gooragoody.
Waterloo: *Illpah.
Waterloo Falls: Bambooyang.
Watsons Bay: Kulli.
Wellingrove: *Eabrai.
Wellington: Wirrum Wirrum.

Wellington, Point: Cullen Cullen.
West Head: Gurugal.
Whiteman's Bridge: *Tunningah.
White's Swamp: *Curringbung.
William, Mount: Weebib.
Wilson's Downfall: *Ooringuldain.
Wilsons Hill: Uloom.
Wingerbourne: Goorambi.

Y

Yates Crossing: Wagengugarra.
Yetholme: Nowendong.
Yimbun: Kannangur.
York: Balladong.
York, Cape: Goodangarkagi.